REMINISCING ALONG THE CONESTOGA

by Lester Burkholder

REMINISCING ALONG THE CONESTOGA

Copyright © 2003

Front Cover
Pioneer Henry and Anna Martin's springhouse on the north bank of the Conestoga River near Route 625. Michael Burkholder's wife, Emma, is a descendant of Pioneer Henry and Anna Martin who lived their entire life on a portion of the land settled by (Creek) Henry Martin.

Library of Congress Control Number: 2003112610

International Standard Book Number: 1-930353-82-0

Published 2003 by
Masthof Press
219 Mill Road
Morgantown, PA 19543-9516

✦ *Contents* ✦

Forward iv
Preface vi

1. Michael Burkholder's Parents and Incidents From His Boyhood 1

2. Martha Burkholder's Legacy 7

3. Conestoga Roller Mill 9

4. The Old Covered Bridge 16

5. The Conestoga Wagons 20

6. John W. Burkholder Purchases Conestoga Roller Mill 23

7. Michael and Emma Burkholder 26

8. Automobiles and the Mennonites 56

9. Conestoga Traction Company 61

10. Trupe's Mill Experiences 65

11. Road Walkers 71

12. Phares Martin's 1926 Mack Truck 77

13. Neighborhood Challenges 80

14. School Problems in the Weaverland Valley 86

15. Church Involvements 92

16. Life's Experiences 96

17. Michael Burkholder's Ancestors 110

• iii •

◆ *Forward* ◆

Some of my favorite boyhood recollections stem from instances when Father and my uncles would reminisce about their boyhood memories and experiences. By reminiscing about happenings in years gone by we can soon see that while many things have changed, some things also stay the same.

I want to express appreciation to all who so willingly shared their memories. First to my father, Raymond Burkholder, whose vivid stories of his youth aroused the desire to record these happenings. His passing in the midst of this project made progress difficult, yet made it keenly evident if these things are to be preserved for future generations, time is of the essence. Thank you to all of my uncles and aunts who willingly shared precious memories. This would also include Uncle Frank, who whenever we met, would invariably turn to his wife, Eva, and exclaim, "Don't tell him anything. He will put it in his book." But with a gentle nudge, he would soon be skipping down memory lane with enthusiasm.

I hardly knew how to handle the "tobacco" issue in this book. In our day and age, we recognize serious health issues with the use of tobacco. This also places an accountability factor on those growing tobacco, with a serious health and spirituality risks to those growing and using it. However, in the period portrayed in this book, these issues were not so readily apparent. There were some in the medical profession who felt tobacco was a deterrent to some diseases, especially tuberculosis and parasites. I have no desire to judge our ancestors on this issue. They were human beings subject to failure, just as we are today. There was a time that I felt they were innocent of the dangers that we now know tobacco involves. However, no student of ancestral study can ignore that in times past, voices rumbled through the Weaverland Valley warning of this "inconsistency." Tobacco was then, and is today, justified as an economic issue, just as slavery was in our forefather's time.

While I do not condone farming or the use of tobacco, or fully grasp how professing Christians today can condone it. However, in this book, the reader will see tobacco treated exactly as the characters viewed it. Farming and using tobacco was an important and accepted part of their life. It was viewed no differently from any of the other crops grown and harvested off the land.

As a young man on one of our visits with elderly Michael Burkholder, the tobacco subject was discussed. He admitted with today's knowledge of the dangers of tobacco, it would be wise to have no part with it. However, he also confessed that for him it was difficult to remain free from its influence.

Whenever a person scrutinizes people and happenings in time past it seems the items most prevalent in one's memory are things of a questionable nature. The author strove to write this in context with Philippians 4: 8: **Finally, brethren, whatsoever things are true, whatsoever things are honest, whatsoever things are just, whatsoever things are pure, whatsoever things are lovely, whatsoever things are of good report; if there be any virtue, and if there be any praise, think on these things**.

When the nature of the "old man" or imperfections of mankind show though, I pray that the reader can also be taught a redeeming virtue in the final outcome of the incident.

This book explores the life, and episodes of our immediate ancestors. It also explores some landmarks which influenced life in the Weaverland Valley. May the reader be inspired, taught, and edified, by the steps our ancestors trod.

- Lester Burkholder

◆ *Preface* ◆

"Whence camest Thou? And wither wilt thou go?"
Genesis 16:8

An individual cannot comprehend how day-to-day decisions and actions will influence the rising generation. Every individual, in every generation, is accountable for his or her own actions, yet their influences reach into following generations. Our ancestors were known for their faith in God. Father worked hard, usually on the farm, to supply the needs of the family. Mother fulfilled her God-given place in the home as a wife and mother. Children were taught Godly virtues, to take responsibility, and to work well at a young age. However, mingled through these everyday happenings a faith was at work. Our ancestors were guiding their children to Jesus Christ, and teaching them Christian virtues by deed and example. Our ancestors walked the Christian walk of life, hoping and praying the next generation would follow. If the Christian walk is lost, it is often lost in the succeeding generations.

"Wither wilt thou go?" . . . certainly a challenge for all of us. Will the Lord find faith in my life and in the life of my descendants when He comes again? Is my life, is your life, an inspiration, an encouragement to others to help them live for God?

• *Chapter One* •

Michael Burkholder's Parents and Incidents From His Boyhood

JOHN W. BURKHOLDER
November 29, 1861 - April 4, 1941
and
SUSAN WENGER
January 2,1865 - August 28,1952

John Burkholder and his wife Susan owned a farmed northeast of the Conestoga Creek where Route 625 crosses today. Trupe's Mill, now gone for the sake of progress, was also in the immediate vicinity.

John, who had the nickname of "Chubby John," was a meticulous farmer. The buildings, fields, fences, yard, and garden, reflected great care in every detail. The big brown sandstone house shaded by large trees reflected the same supervision. An impressive hitching post sent a welcoming message to all.

John appears to have had a chronic respiratory problem, as he always had a large water droplet on the tip of his nose. Sometimes he would forget to blow his nose and his shirt would get wet from his nasal discharge. His grandchildren remember he could not spend much time in the dusty tobacco stripping room until he was coughing and wheezing.

John was a short chunky man from which he derived the nickname "Chubby John." He wore homemade broad fall pants, jackets without labels, and a broad-brimmed brown felt hat as he worked throughout the week. Sunday clothes were of the same pattern, but made of the newest articles of clothing that his wife, Susan, had made. His leathery unshaven face betrayed the evidence of long hard days at work outside in the cold in the winter or in the hot sun in the summer. In his younger years, John trimmed his beard with scissors. The ultra-conservative Mennonites considered shaving worldly.

John's farm buildings were right behind Trupe's Mill. The farm buildings still stand today, even though the mill is gone. Today the location is known as Horst's Nursery. John was a prosperous farmer and kept everything in meticulous condition. His management caused him to prosper and he purchased many neighboring farms as they came available.

Susan had a flock of free-ranging Plymouth Rock chickens to supply eggs for the large family. With Trupe's Mill only a short distance away, there was a constant struggle to keep the chickens home. Who can blame them? Why scrounge around for bugs and such like, if you know there are all kinds of spilled grain a short distance away. These chickens got into the mill, laying their eggs in the nooks and crannies. They also left evidence of their passing, which no self-respecting miller would want his customers to see. Several times a week, Susan or the children would make a thorough search of their neighbor's property for the large brown eggs their chickens had laid.

John Burkholder was a diligent promoter of the German language. He and Susan used a German Bible for their family devotions. The children were expected to audibly read from the German Bible every morning for devotions. When they were stuck on a difficult word, help was not readily offered. The children were expected to sound the word out until it was correct. In this way, the children not only were taught biblical truths, but also learned the German language. This method apparently had its desired results, as their son, Michael, was an avid supporter of the German language all of his life. In Michael's later years, he was asked to lead in an audible prayer. He replied that he prays in German and the rest of the people would not understand it.

On October 3, 1903, there was an ordination held for deacon at Bowmansville Mennonite Church. The lot fell on Samuel Z. Musser, but John W. Burkholder was one of the eight candidates in the lot.

Route 73 approaching John W. Burkholder's farm from the north. The Conestoga Mill and the old covered bridge are also visible.

John grew sweet potato plants for resale. Each spring he had customers coming to purchase his sweet potato plants to plant in their gardens at home. Early one spring morning a young man arrived on horseback to purchase a basketful of John's sweet potato seedlings.

His steed, a handsome, high-spirited sorrel, pranced in the farm lane with magnificent coordination. John's boys, Michael, Daniel, and John, watched as the rider put his steed through a variety of gaits in high-style for his onlookers. After the customer performance had ended, he tied his handsome steed at the family hitching post at the yard fence. Then he followed the boys to the garden to choose the plants he wanted to purchase. The boys soon were picking choice plants, placing them in a basket to transport to their new home. The rider was ready to leave. However, the high-spirited horse did not cooperate. As soon as the man tried to mount with the basket, the horse shied away and reared up on his hind legs. Finally, the rider gave the basket to Michael, and mounted the horse. Michael held up the basket as the horse with its rider cavorted by. However, the horse, still fearful of this strange object, wheeled, snorted, and kicked, hitting Michael on the chest with such force that he flew over

The boyhood home of Michael W. Burkholder as it appears today.

the fence into the yard. The seedlings and the basket landed in the yard near the porch.

Michael, unconscious, was carried into the house and the doctor was called. The doctor's examination revealed three broken ribs and various cuts and bruises. Michael's injuries confined him to bed for a week.

The sweet potato plants were gathered together and placed in the basket. The next morning the young man came again—this time in a buggy with a different horse. He offered to pay for the doctor's bill, but Michael's father, John, refused. He said it was an accident and did not want to lose a customer.

As Michael recuperated from the accident, he received many visitors. Eli and Clayton Gehman, two neighborhood boys, visited Michael. They were the sons of the operator of Conestoga Roller Mill, later called Trupe's Mill, located just across the Conestoga Creek. Eli had an assortment of novels hidden on the top shelf of the corner cupboard in the mill office. Novels were considered worldly reading material. Before Eli left to visit Michael, he would select some novels which he thought might interest Michael and placed them under his shirt. At Michael's bedside, he withdrew them and gave them to Michael.

Michael accepted them, placed them under his pillow, and offered his visitors some "Black Jack" chewing gum. He had ordered, and received this luxury by mail. His sister had snuck it to his bedside, as spending money for chewing gum was considered wasteful. The boys visited for a while, enjoying the companionship, and the chewing gum. When Eli and Clayton came downstairs after their visit, John and Susan thanked the boys for coming and invited them to sit down for cookies and lemonade.

The forbidden gum lay motionless in their mouths, but cookies and lemonade also beckoned. The boys looked at each other, stretched their necks, swallowed, and sat down. The treat was delicious, almost making up for the loss of the forbidden gum.

Three scenes of the mill race and water gate of Conestoga Roller Mill which later was known as Trupe's Mill.

Credit: *100 Years of Camera Scenes.*

• Chapter Two •

Martha Burkholder's Legacy

John's eldest sister, Martha, was well-liked in the community. Since she never married, she was available to help the neighbors whenever a need arose. She also enjoyed visiting the elderly in the community.

After struggling a losing battle with a ten-day bout of pneumonia, she passed away on February 10, 1899, at age 39 years living at home with her parents, Daniel and Anna. The family planned the funeral at Martindale Church. According to some reports, there were two deaths in the community with plans to bury both persons in Martindale's Cemetery in separate ceremonies. But the day before, a severe blizzard swept through the Valley and the grave diggers had a difficult time preparing the burial sites.

On the morning of Martha's funeral, the friends and relatives of Martha had a daunting challenge. The soft and fluffy snow was deeper than the horse's shoulders and a driving wind made traveling extremely difficult. The horse-drawn sleighs just sank into the powdery snow making it impossible for the horses to pull.

Wanting to attend his sister's funeral, John went off to Martindale Church on horseback with a blanket wrapped around himself for protection from the cold and snow. His wife, and the rest of the family remained at home.

Daniel and Anna, Martha's parents, had a neighbor, Martin S. Frey, who was noted for his fine horses. He hooked four of his horses to a wagon and broke a path for the funeral procession from Daniel Burkholder's home to the church. As the team labored, breaking the difficult trail, the deep fluffy snow rolled in on the horses' backs, causing a cloud of steam to rise; but it was swiftly swept away in the blinding wind of the crisp cold air. The severe wind and drifting snow made progress very difficult for all.

Due to the severe weather, most of the women stayed home. The storm also prevented many of Martha's elderly friends from attending the funeral. But Martha's single 32-year-old younger sister, Mary, really wanted to attend the funeral. Most of the mourners traveled on horseback, but John's twenty-year-old younger brother, Daniel, drove his sister, Mary, to the church yard, although the sleigh indignantly upset, dumping its occupants into the snow. When it was time to conduct the grave site services, they shoveled the snow out of the grave before they could lower the coffin into the grave.

After the services, John headed home again. Due to the difficult traveling, he did not arrive home until about dusk. Susan and the children had begun the chores and were beginning to become concerned when he finally arrived. As Susan and the children were returning to the house with a lantern, she saw John arriving home, half frozen, but happy to be home.

But what was Martha's legacy? Martha's funeral set a precedent for Old Order Weaverland Conference which is still followed yet today. During the 1870s and 1880s, the progressive element of the church began to hold funeral services at the church. The traditional method was to hold services at the deceased's home and then proceed to the cemetery for the internment. Time has obliterated all the details of how the conservative Deacon Daniel Burkholder and his family reached a decision to hold Martha's services at Martindale Church. Possibly the severe weather had a bearing on this decision.

What is remembered is that Martha's father, Deacon Daniel Burkholder, requested a service at the home before they departed for the memorial service at the church. This set a precedent. For those desiring a funeral service at church, from this time on, a short service was conducted at the home for the immediate family, then proceeding to the church for internment, followed by another service at church.

When Daniel was challenged about having the funeral service at church, he replied, "Something new which is good is wise to consider."

The years 1900 to 1920 were a transitional period, with about half the funerals conducted only at the home, and the other half both at home and at church. But gradually, the services both at home and at church prevailed, with the precedent set by the funeral of a kindhearted sister of the faith, a request of her father, and a blinding snowstorm.

* *Chapter Three* *

Conestoga Roller Mill

The Conestoga Creek ambles through some of the most fertile land of Lancaster County. Conestoga Roller Mill, later known as Trupe's Mill, was only one of many mills strategically located along the Conestoga River. Conestoga Roller Mill was located south of Terre Hill and Bowmansville. Blue Ball and Goodville was located about one mile south of the mill. The large 35 x 70-foot, four-story, wooden structure dominated the country-side around it. Its pale blue color harmonized with the sparkling Conestoga River flowing alongside it, and pleasingly diverged with the fertile farms around it. A small cabin-like structure perched atop the building housed the head-shaft for the grain elevator. For those who climbed to the top, its four windows provided a panoramic view of the Weaverland Valley.

Judge Thomas Edwards of Spring Grove was an early owner of the land where the mill stood. However, he carefully guarded the water rights on the Conestoga River. Nevertheless, on May 7, 1744, he granted a deed to his Mennonite and pioneer neighbors, Henry Martin and Christian Schneder, to build a dam across the Conestoga to convey water in a ditch in order to irrigate his fields. This deed restricted Henry Martin and Christian Schnader from using this dam or ditch for any purposes except irrigating his lands.

Why did Henry Martin and Christian Schnader desire water rights from their adjoining neighbors' land, when the Conestoga ran right through their own properties? The answer can be seen when a person studies the path of the Conestoga. Its course through Henry Martin and Christian Schnader properties was relatively straight. However, just upstream the Conestoga made a large sweeping oxbow, and by placing a ditch across this oxbow, a person could benefit from a much greater rise in the river in a much shorter distance.

Judge Thomas Edwards also recognized this and reserved the rights to draw water from the Conestoga above the dam, directing this water over his lands and discharging it back into the Conestoga below the dam and Henry Martin's farming enterprise. Judge Thomas Edwards apparently had plans for a water-powered enterprise, but he passed away in 1764 at age 91 before he could fulfill this goal.

About ten years after Judge Edwards' death, James Lardner began digging a race for a sawmill. The Revolutionary War interrupted his plans, and after peace and prosperity returned to the Valley this tract of land was sold to Henry Weaver. He erected a gristmill in 1787 using this partly-completed ditch as his millrace. The planned sawmill was also apparently built as early maps show a water-powered sawmill located on the same race as the gristmill. All traces of the sawmill have long disappeared.[1] From about 1851 to 1876, the mill was also known Weaver Mills Post Office with Miller John Weaver as postmaster.

The mill was water-powered, created by twin turbines spinning deep in the bowels of the mill. When the mill was in operation, it had a restful, humming sound, sort of a comforting tenor created by the feel and tone of smoothly-running machinery. Bell, the wife of Samuel O. Trupe, would take her fretting babies out in the mill and they were soon fast asleep.

A dusting of pure white flour would settle everywhere, scenting the air and mingling with the sweet aroma of fresh corn meal. When stepping into the mill, you could almost taste the products produced there. This, along with the steady flow of customers, made life at the mill quite fascinating. It was not uncommon to have five or six teams patiently waiting to unload their grain, while the drivers visited under the shade tree. The mill was the community source of the latest news and also had a counter where treats could be purchased by children and their parents. Whenever farm work would slow down, or on a rainy day, or in the slow season, the Conestoga Roller Mill became the gathering spot for the

---

[1] M[artin] G. Weaver, *Mennonites of the Lancaster Conference*. Scottdale, Pa.: Mennonite Publishing House, 1931.

Dam for the Conestoga Roller Mill. The water level below the dam is higher now because another obstruction has been placed below the dam to provide a fording place for farm machinery.

neighborhood "philosophers." Many of the world's problems would have been solved in the Mill office, if only the politicians of those days would have heeded their advice.

All of the wheat and other feed ingredients delivered to the mill had to be carried to the upper two stories of the mill. There they began their journey through the milling process. A hoist lifted the wheat and other ingredients up to the upper stories. Outside of the mill, up at the peak of the gable end of the roof, protruded an extension, in which a hoist apparatus was installed. This hoist was water-powered by a shaft that continuously ran as long as the turbines were turning. A long rope with a short piece of chain on the end, reached to the ground. There was a strategically-located door on each story of the mill where this rope traveled up and down outside the mill. Just inside the door was a hoist control rope which also extended down through all the mill's floors. This control rope would engage the hoist when pulled. The harder it was pulled, the faster the hoist would lift. With a feather touch, 300 pounds of bagged feed could be made to dangle at any level from the ground up to the peak of the mill roof.

When a load of wheat would arrive, the farmer would park his wagon under the hoist. The mill worker, standing at the door high above, would lower the hoist rope and chain to the wagon bed below. The farmer laid the chain on his wagon bed and laid two or three bags of wheat over the chain. When the chain encircling the bags was securely fastened, the mill worker pulled the control rope right inside the door. This tightened a belt high in the mill, engaging the hoist, and lifting the wheat to where he was waiting. When the wheat reached the door where the mill worker stood, he would let the wheat rise up to where he could grasp it with one hand, with the other hand controlling the hoist. When he had a good grip on the dangling bags, he would slightly release his pull on the hoist control rope and pull the bags of wheat in on the mill floor to down at his feet. The mill worker would let the rope down to the farmer for the next load and carry the delivered bag to their storage place.

Many tons of feed were delivered and stored in this manner. Some ingredients, like cottonseed, came to the East Earl train station by the twenty-ton freight car load. There the bags were unloaded from the rail car onto horse-drawn wagons, and later trucks, and brought to the mill. The mill also purchased wheat and other feed ingredients in bulk, which was delivered to the East Earl train station. These ingredients were bagged by hand and hauled to Conestoga Roller Mill by teams. Then the bags were elevated to the upper levels of the mill by the hoist, and stored until milled into flour or animal feed.

While Conestoga Roller Mill was considered a flourmill, it also manufactured animal feed for the local farmers. The farmers could bring their own home-grown grains to the mill in 100-pound bags. Pulling their horse and wagon and later their trucks under the hoist at the gable end of the mill to be unloaded, their corn was hoisted to the upper levels of the mill to be ground and blended into animal feed. The farmers would then pull to a side door and pick up the manufactured animal feed.

Two water-powered turbines powered Trupe's Mill. A canal of water the length of 1,300 feet, supplied the mill's turbines with water. A five-foot high dam created this canal of still, but powerful water, upstream from the mill. There were water gates at the upper and lower

Original water gate which controlled the water into the mill race.

ends of the millrace. The millrace ran right up under the mill. Just before it arrived at the mill, a channel turned left toward the Conestoga River where there was a water gate. Any excess water not used to spin the turbine powering the mill fell over this gate and flowed back to the river. Large wheels, which opened water gates, were used to empty the millrace. A narrow plank crossed the race at this point, which was an attraction to all the daring youth in the area.

The millrace was an attraction for all. With swimming in the summer, and ice-skating in the winter, the millrace drew the area youth like a magnet. Fishing in deep cool water was another attraction for many. Sunnies, suckers, catfish, and carp thrived in the still water. It had a variety of wildlife: bullfrogs, birds, turtles, and other wild animals inhabitated its banks. Snakes were common, and if caught, added a variety of thrills for both the boys and girls.

Many of the great-grandparents of those reading this account may have become acquainted while boating on the millrace. The courting couples in years past enjoyed many evenings boating under the shade of the tree-lined millrace. In the still of the evening, as the dusk deepened, and the moon rose in awesome magnificence, many a marriage proposal was interrupted by an occasional croak of a bullfrog.

The mill also had a huge Fairbanks Morse, one cylinder, 25 HP, slow-speed diesel engine that provided power when the water was low, or when trouble developed with the turbines. When it was running, the sharp burst of its exhaust pierced the tranquil sounds of the peaceful country-side. When the mill was running at full capacity the waterpower was insufficient.

In the prime years of the mills' operation, there were times, right after the wheat harvest, that the mill ran continuously from Monday morning until Saturday night. The diesel operated day and night during these times. The starting procedure was very complicated. First, the operator took a torch and heated a knob on the engine's head until it glowed cherry red. (Then, pulling on the diesel's enormous man-high flywheel in the direction it was to be run until the operator felt the compression in it, a huge piston pulled the flywheel to a stop.) The operator would then jump on the spokes of the large flywheel to spin the engine in the opposite direction of it's intended rotation as hard as he could. This caused the engine to spin into the compression cycle backwards. A man could not generate enough momentum to bring the engine to go over center. However, enough compression in the cylinder was produced that the recoil caused the engine to rebound in the opposite direction, the way it was supposed to run, that with some additional help, enough momentum was created to send it over center, fire, and run. Occasionally, the engine would not fire on the first rebound, but instead on the second; therefore, it would be running backwards. The engine would have to be shut down, and the whole procedure repeated to get it running in the right direction.

Occasionally, the mud and debris had to be removed from the millrace. The mill operator would go to the head of the race at the dam where the water entered the canal from the Conestoga River and close the gates. Opening the waste gate would let the water already in the race flow into the Conestoga. This was done in the evening when the mill was shut down for the day. This also brought the neighborhood together because of the large amount of fish which were easily gigged as the water level went down. They had no way of escape. The men and boys all came with their pitchforks and speared the trapped fish in the bottom of the millrace. Many of these fish found their way to the neighborhood's kitchen tables.

After the millrace was cleaned of the large debris, the mill operator would open the gate supplying the water to the race slightly causing a small stream of water to flow through the race. Hitching a mule to a field harrow, he would stir up the mud and sediment in the millrace, which would then be washed out the waste gate.

At the turn of the century, there was a problem of large eels entering the mill's turbine and hindering the water flow. This meant that there was not enough power available to operate the mill. If enough of the carcasses were entangled in the mill's turbine, the mill had to shut down and the race emptied. Then a person had to go down and clear the turbine.

The mill house, covered with gray slate shingles, stood near the bank of the millrace, about a hundred feet east of the mill. A grand porch graced the side of the house facing the mill. The mill house faced the millrace. An attached addition contained a laundry, creamery, a large tool shop, and a massive stove oven. The tool shops, laundry, and creamery were water-powered. A water wheel powered from the water rushing down a small sluiceway from the millrace race was located directly across the millrace from the house. Continuous power was transmitted to the workshop attic by a cable. There it drove a pulley and shaft apparatus, which then powered machinery below by an arrangement of belts and pulleys.

A woodshed, painted red like all the outbuildings, stood directly upstream from the mill. The woodshed was built on posts and extended out over the millrace. Its windows provided an excellent opportunity to spend an afternoon fishing on rainy days. The mills blue flat-bottom boat was moored under the woodshed

The barn stood at the end of the lane, which ran between the millrace and the house. Directly across the barnyard, a footbridge arched across the millrace where a large chicken house was located.

• *Chapter Four* •

The Old Covered Bridge

Just downstream from the Conestoga Roller Mill stood a beautiful covered bridge built in 1846. It was one of the early bridges over the Conestoga River. In earlier years, travelers had to ford the river. This was inconvenient and dangerous when the river was running strong. At times, teams and wagons were washed downstream and lives lost when teamsters became impatient. When the bridge was built, it was the only bridge over the Conestoga River between the Paxton Road, "Hinkletown," and Morgantown, a distance of thirteen miles.[2]

When the traffic crossed the covered bridge, you could tell by the noise whether is was a heavy wagon or a buggy. When a heavy wagon with large steel rimed wheels and big draft horses crossed, the heavy floor planks of the bridge would rumble like thunder. A horse and buggy pattered across the bridge with a pleasing resonance.

The timbers and arches and the rafters in the roof formed a climbing enclosure for the young boys of the area. Many Sunday afternoons were spent in the dusky dark confines of the covered bridge roof watching the unsuspecting travelers below; maybe even suppressing an occasional snicker, as a courting couple passed below. If a person who was known to be over-reactive was crossing the bridge, they might suddenly be startled to see a boy hanging from the bottom cord of the rafters right in front of their buggy window. At the last instant, the boyish figure would disappear up in the dark confines of the roof and wait to see the reaction.

---

[2] M[artin] G. Weaver, *Fords and Bridges, Across the Conestoga from Morgantown to Hinkletown.*

Concrete bridge which replaced the covered bridge. The home in the background was John W. Burkholder's retirement home, now owned by his great-grandson, Harold Burkholder. Credit: *100 Years of Camera Scenes.*

In 1914, this covered bridge came under scrutiny of the highway engineers. It was located on the main artery between Reading and Lancaster The road was called the Bowmansville Road, and later was changed to Route 73. Today it is known as Route 625. Since Route 222 was still far in the future, this was the main road between Reading and Lancaster. The highway engineers evaluated the old weather-beaten structure which had served the community for many years, and decided to replace it with a new concrete bridge. Finally, the day arrived that the demolition crew found shelter in the mill. With a blast of dynamite, a cloud of smoke, flying boards, and cracked timbers, the bridge was gone. The grayish boards, the warped shingles, and the graceful weight-bearing arches which carried the weight of thousands of travelers across the Conestoga was gone forever.

Then workers with big tools and screaming saws moved in. They built shacks on the banks of the Conestoga River to store their tools and eat lunch. A guard called Big Nick slept in one of these shacks. Big trucks brought heavy loads of lumber, stone, sand, steel, and cement. The steam engines and concrete mixers ran day and night. In a few months a strong new concrete bridge stood where the old covered bridge had been.

Today this bridge is also gone, replaced by a wider bridge. The earlier bridge was a one-lane affair with high concrete sides. This bridge

Steam engine used to build a new concrete bridge.
Credit: *100 Years of Camera Scenes.*

plays a key role in one of my early recollections of Grandfather. I can vividly recall sitting on Grandpa Michael Burkholder's front porch, visiting on a Sunday afternoon in 1956. He had just built his new retirement home, located about a fourth of a mile south of this bridge. The road passing his home was smooth and straight where it narrowed to one lane to cross the bridge.

  We were peaceably visiting together on the porch, when a black 1955, two-door Chevrolet, and a Baby Blue 1956 Ford Fairlane two-door hardtop (with the continental spare tire kit) glided to a stop. Both cars idled, side by side, directly in front of Michael's house. The sunlight sparkled off the Ford's fender mirrors, and the dual spotlights tucked in front of the doorposts. A pair of big black and white fuzzy dice dangled from the rear-view mirror The rear wheel side skirts gave the car a long low-slung streamlined appearance.

  In youthful innocence, I had no idea what was about to take place, but was busy checking these cars out. Some of the younger uncles, also sitting on the porch, lounging back on the rear two legs of the kitchen chairs, suddenly snapped front and took an avid interest on what was happening out on the highway. The conversation came to a sudden halt as total attention was given to the two cars idling, side-by-side, out on the highway. Michael just sat with a deliberated frown staring in the distance.

The passenger leaned out of the Ford window, which was in the left or passing lane, and shouted, "One, Two, Three, **Go**." Instantly, two V8's screamed, tires screeched, smoke poured from under of the fender skirts, and they were off. (This was an assault on the senses of an eight-year-old boy who had never dreamed it was even possible.) The four exhausts trumpeting the harmonious rap of Hollywood mufflers, merged with the shrill howl of open intakes, as the two cars raced down the road side by side. A fourth of a mile down the road was the one-lane concrete bridge. There was certainly not room for two cars side by side. The decision of which car was the fastest had to be made by the time the cars reached it.

The outcome? Which was the fastest? The Ford or the Chevy? The onlookers on the porch will never know. From our position on the porch, Michael's parlor room blocked the view to the bridge. A step out into the lawn would have provided an excellent view of the outcome. However, all visiting on the porch that afternoon recognized Michael's silent disapproval of such proceedings.

Although the "Uncles" and the nephew, were vividly interested and curious, no one stepped off the porch out of respect to Michael's silent, yet stern, disapproval. The calm peaceful sounds of the Weaverland Valley slowly returned. The conversation continued as if nothing had happened. Somehow, we have slipped a century and half forward. Let us return to slower earlier years gone by.

◆ *Chapter Five* ◆

The Conestoga Wagons

The main mode of transporting commerce at the turn of the century was the Conestoga wagon pulled by six impressive draft horses. The larger Conestoga wagons were loaded with up to ten tons of products and with a full team stretched up to sixty feet long. The sight and sound of six large 1,800-pound draft horses with their bells a-ringing, pulling a blue and vermilion colored Conestoga wagon caught the attention of many a boy.

The Conestoga Valley was also important to four large impressive breed of draft horses. The horse's powerful body gave it stamina, and the large, but relatively short, legs made it ideal for heavy pulling. The Conestoga Draft Horse, also sometimes called the Lancaster Draft Horse, was an ideal animal for heavy wagons. These horses were rarely used on the farm because its large feet were a hindrance when working with valuable crops. They also required more care than mules, which were typically used on the farm.

The Conestoga wagon also had its roots in the Conestoga Valley. An old wheelwright's property is located just upstream from the Conestoga Roller Mill, where Cedars Creek flows into the Conestoga. In 1864, Gideon Weaver owned this property where he manufactured Conestoga wagons until late in the century. Mathias Shirk had originally built it in 1813. However, it was used only a short time when it burned with all its contents.[3] It was rebuilt and became the most extensive (heavy wagon build-

---

[3] M[artin] G. Weaver, *Mennonites of the Lancaster Conference*. Scottdale, Pa.: Mennonite Publishing House, 1931.

Conestoga Wagon Wheel Shop located near the Conestoga River just off Turkey Farm Road was built in 1813 and destroyed by fire in 1848. It was rebuilt by Gideon Weaver and used as a wheelwright shop—the only water-powered wheelwright shop in Lancaster County, Pennsylvania.

ing) shop in eastern Lancaster County. This historic building still stands today and the ruins of the water wheel and some of its line shafts are still visible to those who venture into the dusky confines of this historical building.

Most of Gideon Weaver's "ships of inland commerce," as the Conestoga wagons were sometimes called, were used to take the products produced by the forges, furnaces, and iron mine in eastern Lancaster County to their markets. The Conestoga wagons were not all identical. The cargo of Gideon Weaver's clients did not require the deep swell of the body. A wagon hauling hogsheads would require a deep swell in the body to keep the load from shifting. The size of the wheels was also variable. Generally, the rougher the road the teamster traveled, the larger the wheel he specified since larger wheels rolled much easier than small ones.

Scattered through the Conestoga Valley, there were numerous wheelwrights and wagon makers who manufactured this valuable equipment. From 1750 to about 1900, they were the railroad's main competitors in commerce. The teamsters using the Conestoga wagons were slower, but they were cheaper than the railroad, and offered door-to-door delivery.

The profession of teamster was a hard and rough life. They were gone for weeks on end. A trip from Lancaster to Philadelphia was a five-day journey. Meals and lodging were available at numerous taverns and inns along the main road, but many teamsters preferred to sleep in the wagon. However, the horses came first when they stopped for the night. The horses were unhooked and the feed box was removed from the rear of the wagon and fastened to the tongue in front of the wagon. Then the six horses were fed from either side of the feed box. The horses were also given the opportunity to drink from the huge limestone water trough strategically located along the road and at the taverns. The horses were hobbled and allowed to graze or placed in a large fenced-in area provided by the tavern. If there was a chance of freezing weather, the Conestoga wagons were pulled on planks so that the wheels would not be frozen in the mud the next morning.

Many of these teamsters hauled flour from Trupe's Mill to their customers. At the turn of the century, the new-fangled truck started to replace the Conestoga wagon. Soon the Conestoga wagons were gone, only to be remembered in the minds of the old timers.

• *Chapter Six* •

John W. Burkholder Purchases Conestoga Roller Mill

In 1917, the Unites States declared war on Germany. Suddenly a cloud of apprehension appeared over the Weaverland Valley. Will the boys have to take military training and go to war? The winter of 1918 brought a flu epidemic to the valley. Many funerals were held that winter. The war and the flu epidemic were the standard topic of conversation that winter. The war also bought government agents to the mill with directives to manufacture flour for the government. The owner complied, but placed the mill up for sale. In the spring of 1919, John and Susan Burkholder purchased the Conestoga Mill.

John W. Burkholder hired two Hurst brothers to operate his mill. These two brothers were not as sober-minded as John would have desired and went about their duties singing and whistling. John, a conservative Mennonite, did not appreciate this lighthearted attitude—especially since they whistled and sang in English. John was a staunch supporter of the German language and let this be known to his tenants. This issue came to the forefront one day when John was in the neighboring field cultivating corn with his one-horse cultivator. The cultivator wheel was in need of grease, and it protested each revolution with a resounding squeak. The Hurst brothers were working in the mill and finally one of them ambled over to John. As he approached, John gave the command " Whoa" and the horses, and the offensive squeak came to a halt.

The Hurst brother asked John, "Is that squeak in German or English?"

Painting of Trupe's Mill.

"Giddap," came the reply from John, and he continued cultivating. The Hurst brother never did find out if Burkholder's wheel squeaked in German or English.

In 1923, John rented the mill to Samuel O. Trupe for an annual rent of $1,000.00. During the years of the depression, when times were hard, John dropped the annual rent to $800.00. Up to this point, the mill was first known as the Conestoga Grist Mill, then as Conestoga Roller Mill, but in later years as Trupe's Mill, named for its operator. Trupe operated the mill until 1971, a span of 48 years. From 1923 until 1940, he specialized in producing flour. Trupe purchased eight to ten thousand bushels of wheat from the local farmers and stored it in the mill. Once the wheat was milled into flour, it was transported and sold in New York and Philadelphia. At peak times, the mill was in operation day and night. At peak production, the mill produced 200 pounds of flour an hour.

As John grew older, he enjoyed sitting in the mill office, visiting with the customers and anyone else who was there. His dog usually came along and lay in the corner of the office. One day the dog warden stopped in and noticed that the dog lying in the corner did not have the required license. He asked who owned the dog. John Burkholder remarked, "Just a dog who hangs around the mill." This answer did not satisfy the warden and he persisted until John admitted it was his dog. After the warden left, John remarked that he is still ahead. The fine did not cost as much as the annual dog license would have cost for all the years he had the dog.

In 1936, electric power came to the Weaverland Valley. Trupe's Mill was the most prominent business establishment in the valley. To justify the expense of running an electric line, the Power Company needed a commitment from Trupe's Mill before they would extend the line. Sam Trupe, the operator of the mill, was interested; but John Burkholder, the owner of the mill, was reluctant. For an ultra-conservative horse and buggy Mennonite, this was a conflict. After many visits by many neighbors who wanted to see electricity come to the area, John finally relented to electrify in the mill. Yet, he never hooked his home to the electric line, although it ran right past his front porch.

The processing of grains for animal feed was trending upward. With electric power now available, John Burkholder also upgraded the mill with some electric-powered equipment. He installed a cob breaker, plate mill, and a feed mixer, all powered by electric for his tenant. The rest of the mill was still powered by water or the large diesel. As the project progressed, John remarked that if he had known how much this project was going to cost, he would not have started.

Obviously, John was an astute businessman. He had many business dealings with private individuals and businesses in the community. These private agreements were typed, and made official by a witness. When the Terre Hill Bank went bankrupt during the depression, John and Susan had $40,000 in savings or stocks invested in the Terre Hill Bank. They lost all of it. This was at a time when farms were worth about $10,000 each. Yet, they were able to absorb this loss and go on in life with no change in their lifestyle.

• *Chapter Seven* •

Michael and Emma Burkholder

Michael Burkholder married Emma M. Weaver on November 23, 1922. They started farming and keeping house at one of his father, John W. Burkholder's farms. It was located across the Conestoga River and across the road from the home farm where Michael was born and raised.

Michael and Emma before they were married.

The Bride and Groom Go Visiting

Right after Michael and Emma were married, they spent a week visiting their married brothers and sisters, usually staying for dinner and supper. The bride and groom usually received wedding gifts during these visits. When they were visiting Michael's sister, Magdalena, who was married to David Horning, they gained some insight into the excitement that married life can bring.

The adults were visiting in the kitchen, the children were playing on the floor, and David Horning's infant son, Aaron, was laid in the cradle. Suddenly the baby went into convulsions, probably because he was teething. Everyone rushed to help. They placed cold wash clothes on Aaron's head and feet. Despite their best efforts, they could not stop the convulsions. They called the doctor. He dropped everything and came immediately. Finally, the doctor got Aaron over his problem, but it came right back again. Seven times they thought he was better, but the convulsions returned. Finally, they got Aaron over it and he rested peaceably, lying on the sofa, although all worn out. When the excitement was all over, Emma commented, "If this is married life, I'm having second thoughts on it." If she had known the excitement that seven boys would bring into her life in the near future, she probably would have joined Aaron on the sofa.

Michael and Emma apparently rented or farmed on shares until 1927. On June 20, 1927, John and Michael entered into an agreement that Michael would take full responsibility for the farm. They agreed on a purchase price of $13,750 for the property. Michael and Emma had $4,000 to invest into the farm. His father agreed to let the remaining money in the farm at four percent annual interest due on April 1. The transfer of the deed was to transpire when the farm was half paid.

The actual deed for the farm was transferred on December 31,1936, almost ten years later. At the time the deed was transferred, a balance of $1400 remained, which was paid June 1937.

Emma was the daughter of Frank M. Weaver, who owned land on which Phares Martin, and later Ivan Martin, operated a stone quarry. Frank received a royalty of ten cents a ton for every load of stone leaving the quarry. The quarry was prosperous and this benefited Frank financially.

Michael and Emma were regularly gifted some of these funds, as they were paying on their farm.

With this outside help, Michael made substantial financial progress on his farm as he made regular payments to his father. John was not aware his son was receiving funds from his father-in-law. However, John was not above going to Rufus Horst and David Horning, who were renting other farms he owned, and point out Michael's progress. Unwittingly, he was promoting his son's abilities to his other tenants, but they were at a definite disadvantage, not having another source of income.

Early History on Michael and Emma's Farm

The farm that Michael and Emma purchased has a rich history in the Anabaptist settlement of Weaverland. It was part of 153 acres which was surveyed for thirty-year-old immigrant Henry Martin in 1733. He and his wife Anna (Oberholtzer) and five small children had arrived in Philadelphia on September 21, 1731, aboard the ship *Britannia*. He was known as Hans Heinrich Martin, and later called "Creek Henry" Martin. Henry and his bother, David, came to America, with the approval of their father, Christian, who was in jail in Europe because of his faith. About two years later, after Christian was released, he also came to Weaverland.

Henry and Anna chose a spot near a spring up on a bluff on the north side of the Conestoga to erect a crude log cabin. Log cabins were eventually replaced with double-stone houses with an adjoining roof over both sections which created a combined porch. The spot that Henry and Anna had chosen for their home was just across the Conestoga River from the home his great-great-great-granddaughter Emma, and her new husband, Michael were moving into 191 years later. All of Michael and Emma's farm was part of the original 153-acre plantation that Henry and Anna settled on in 1731.

An early map reveals Old State Road (now Route 625) as the boundary line to the east of the original tract of land. The original farm extended almost to today's Goodwill Store. In the other direction, Henry's farm lay to the road which is known today as Long Lane. The Conestoga River flowed right through the property and the rich low lying fields just

• 28 •

Michael and Emma Burkholder's farm in 2003, now owned by Norman Hahn.

north of the Conestoga River were the choice farming spots on the farms of both Henry Martin and his neighbor to the west, Christian Schnader. This led to the deed granting them the right to build a dam across the Conestoga to convey water in a ditch to irrigate his fields. This dam was on the neighbor Judge Thomas Edwards's property, and restricted Henry Martin and Christian Schnader from using this dam or ditch for any purposes except irrigating their lands as mentioned earlier.

    Henry and Anna's son, also called Henry, sometimes called "Creek Henry" II, married Barbara Zimmerman in 1765. The story has been handed down through the generations that one day while Barbara was working in the house, some Indians arrived and demanded some whiskey. Barbara refused and told the Indians to leave, threatening to shout to the men in the barn for help. In reality, she knew she was alone. The threat worked, and the Indian left with no whiskey.[4]

    Henry and Barbara purchased the complete 153-acre homestead tract from his father on October 19, 1765. Henry, Sr., remained living in one side of the double-stone homes after his son purchased the homestead.

---

[4] H. K. Martin.

Original deed granted to Pioneer Henry Martin on January 10, 1733. Henry paid £23 and 14 shillings for 153 acres of land with an allowance for six acres of roads and highways.

Henry, Jr., also had a serious scrape with the famous General George Washington. The tentacles of the strife caused by Revolutionary War reached into the Weaverland Valley. The Mennonite leanings during this conflict usually were neutral, not getting directly involved. They did not join the patriotic zeal of the revolutionary cause, but neither did they aid the loyalist efforts. This created a fine line in the public's eyes between neutrality and a disguised Tory.

James Bart, a British soldier, was captured January 17, 1781, by Revolutionary soldiers, and was imprisoned as a prisoner of war in a stockade in the city of Lancaster. Over a year later, on September 7, 1782, he and two other British soldiers escaped from their captors. Their goal was to unite with their fellow British soldiers who had been captured and were residing in New York City. Apparently, their escape route took them through the Weaverland Valley where they received assistance. Henry O. Martin, along with two other Mennonite neighbors gave the escaped prisoners, meat, drink, lodging, clothing, and other necessities for their journey to New York. This was not done with a patriotic motive, but simply one human being helping another with his needs.

However, not everyone viewed it this way. On October 15, 1782, the Supreme Court of the State of Pennsylvania convened at Lancaster. At this hearing, Henry O. Martin was indicted,[5] convicted, and placed in jail, by a jury of the county residents, of "basely and treacherously helping an enemy of the United States of America." He was fined £50,[6] payable before March 1, 1783. If he could not pay this stiff fine, or chose not to, he would be publicly whipped with 39 lashes at the Lancaster whipping post.

The neighbors of the jailed Mennonites presented an appeal of the peaceable character of their neighbor, which was read in court, but it appeared to be ignored. Finally, Peter Miller of the Ephrata Cloisters who had translated the *Martyrs Mirror* from Dutch to German, came to their aid. Peter Miller was a friend of General George Washington. Peter Miller pleaded that these men were not guilty of treason, but they simply followed the scriptures teachings, "If thine enemy hunger, feed him." Peter Miller's appeal was hand-delivered by Henry Martin's Mennonite brethren to Philadelphia only a month before the deadline for payment or whipping. As a result, General George Washington pardoned Henry Martin and his two neighbors of their jail sentences and greatly reduced their fines.[7]

Henry and Barbara's eldest daughter, Anna (1764-1842), married Henrich Rutt. They settled on the north side of the Conestoga where Michael and Emma's farm is located. They possibly started homesteading where the buildings are today. There is no record that the homestead was subdivided at this time, or that it was ever divided in their name.[8]

---

[5] Eli D. Wenger and George G. Sauder. *The Weaverland Mennonites*. Manheim, Pa., Authors, 1968.; Richard K. MacMaster, *Conscience in Crisis: Mennonites and Other Peace Churches in America, 1739-1789*. Scottdale, Pa.: Mennonite Publishing House, 1979.

[6] Henry had purchased his 153-acre farm for £266, which gives an idea as to how steep this fine was.

[7] Richard K. MacMaster. *Conscience in Crisis*.

[8] Wenger and Sauder, p. 222, #64.

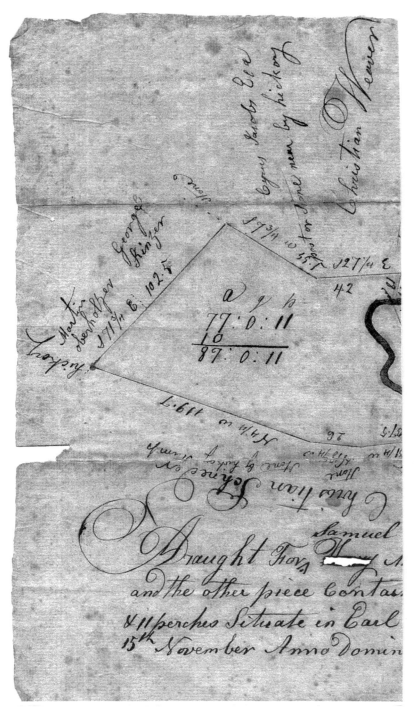

Half of the document (other half on next page) showing the . .

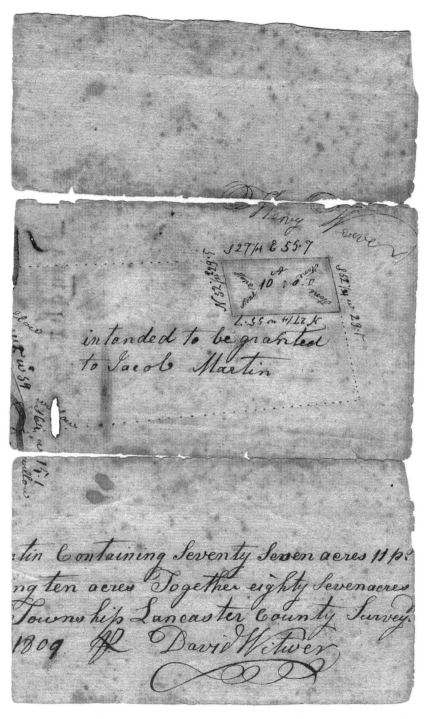

... division of Henry Martin's farm to his sons Jacob and Samuel.

The pioneer homestead farm went to Henry and Barbara's younger sons, Samuel and Jacob. In 1809, a map was drafted specifying that Jacob was to receive the portion of the farm south of the Conestoga River. Samuel was the great-grandfather of Emma; thus, at this point, the home and farm Michael and Emma were starting to housekeep moved outside of Emma's direct linage. However, the farm stayed in the Martin family for two more generations. Jacob's youngest son, Henry "saw miller," was the next owner. The fifth generation of Martins to own this farm was "saw miller," Henry Martin's son Elisha.[9] Nathan Diller purchased the farm in 1876. Well respected Preacher Frank W. Hurst moved there about 1894, and paid $7,000 for the farm, which was extremely high for that time.[10]

Michael's father, John, purchased this property from Preacher Frank W. Hurst in 1913 for $12,700, and gave his son the opportunity to farm it. Michael and Emma raised their family, and lived on this property all their lives.

It is doubtful Michael and Emma had any idea of their farm's rich ancestral Anabaptist history and the direct ties it had to Emma's forefathers. If they did, they never spoke of it.

The Family Grows

The Lord blessed Michael and Emma with children. Melvin was born in 1924. Twenty-two months later, Raymond, my father, joined the little family. Michael Lloyd was born in 1927.

Michael and Emma took their family responsibility seriously. Michael read the Bible audibly to his family every morning, usually right after breakfast. Emma taught the children a small rhyming prayer in the German language. Translated to English, it loses it rhythm, but it went like this:

> *I am little*
> *My heart is pure*
> *No one can live in it*
> *But Jesus Christ alone.*

---

[9] Old property deeds; Lloyd W. Burkholder.
[10] *Descendants of Frank W. Hurst, 1863-2000*

Public Sale.

On SATURDAY, the 9th day of FEBUARY, 1856,

Will be sold at public sale, at the residence of the undersigned, in East Earl Township, Lancaster County; 1 mile west of Spring Grove Forge, near John Wever's Mill; the following personal property, to wit:—

1 Horse, 2 Cows,

1 Narrow-wheeled plantation Wagon, a one horse Wagon.

4 SETS OF HARNESS.

FARMING UTENSILS &C.

2 Ploughs, 1 Harrow, 1 Shovel-Harrow, 1 pair of Wood ladders, 1 Wheelbarrow, 2 Jackscrews, 2 Crosscut Saws, 1 Sleigh, 1 Ladder 30ft. in length. 3 Log Chains. Forks, Rakes, Shovels, Spades, Hoes, &c.

LUMBER.

A lot of Walnut inch boards and 2in. planks, 1000ft. of half inch Poplar boards. Oak plank of every size and description, Ash and Hickory plank, sawed Hickory axel-trees, sawed Posts, Rails and Pails for fance.

Househld and Kitchen Furniture, &c.

1 Kitchen dresser, 1 corner Cubboard, 2 Bedsteads and Bedding, Tables and Chairs, 1 Copper Kettle, 1 small Brass Kettle, Pots and Pans, a Seine 18ft. in length and other Fish nets, a double barrel Gun, Apples, Potatoes, &c. With a variety of other articles to numerous to insert,

☞ *SALE to commence at* **12** *o'clock* (**M.**) *Terms made known oy*

HENRY MARTIN,

(sawmiller.)

December 31, 1855.

JOSEPH SHIRK, *Printer, Turkey Hill, Lancaster County, Pa.*

*Sale bill of a farm sale held on Michael's farm
on February 9, 1856, by saw miller Henry Martin.*

The children learned obedience at an early age. When Raymond was a toddler, he committed a misdeed, and was reprimanded. He was vehemently crying, not fully submitting to parental authority. Suddenly a big smile came to his face as he announced, "I am not angry anymore," and became a cheerful child again. Parental authority was taught, and accepted, early in life.

As a preschooler, Raymond was helping Michael in the tobacco stripping room. Apparently, the time was long for Raymond because he asked his father, "Is it time for dinner?"

Michael replied with his usual answer, "We will put another 'go' through." Another "go" was Michael's term for another trip to the damp tobacco cellar for a large handful of lath filled with tobacco stalks. These stalks were stripped of their leaves and placed in a bale

Raymond asked this question numerous times through the week, and Michael always had the same answer. On Sunday, Michael was sitting in church with his two little boys beside him. The preaching portion of the service was over, and the congregation had sung one of the two songs usually sung. In the lull between songs, Raymond asked his father, "Is it time to go home?"

Michael shook his head and Raymond audibly remarked, "We will put another 'go' through," and settled back contently.

Daily Life

Keeping a working family of growing boys fed and clothed was no small task. The farm was mostly self-sufficient. The cows provided milk; the chickens, eggs; and the meat was homegrown and then butchered. A large lush garden provided vegetables for the table. Trips to the grocery store were infrequent.

Every fall, early in the morning, Clarence Renninger came to the farm to choose four or five pigs to butcher. Clarence took the homegrown pigs to his butcher shop in Spring Grove to butcher and process the meat. Michael said Clarence's puddins' were the best around. Fried corn meal, mush and puddins', a mixture of corn meal, beef, and pork meat scraps, was the breakfast staple in the Burkholder household. Clarence also made pork sausage that was common fare.

The pigs were raised heavy by today's standards, which also made the meat very fatty. Seven to eight hundred pounds pigs were common with each producing five cans of lard. Michael also took charge of curing the hams. He would line up the hams on a bench in the summer kitchen and regularly baste them with Morton's Sugar Cure. After about two months of careful, consistent basting, the hams were cured to Michael's expectations. He then told the boys to wash them off, usually with used rags. They placed the hams up in the house attic where they would hang, providing a delightful odor. According to Michael's boys, they have not tasted hams to this day that equal those home-cured hams.

Another chore that went with butchering was the unpleasant task of making soap. The fat was brought home from the butcher shop, and rendered to make soap for the family. They heated the fat in the tubs used to heat wash water until it was a liquid.

A mixture of lye, borax, and water was also prepared. The lye mixture was added to cold water, which created a chemical reaction, which heated the water. This was mildly dangerous, as it would cause a chemical burn if accidentally applied to the skin.

The lye mixture was slowly stirred into the hot fat with a wooden paddle and then left to cool. About every hour, it had to be stirred; and as it cooled, the soap mixture would thicken and lighten. By the next morning, it would be white and hard and Emma would slice the soap into squares. She would use this soap to wash dishes and clothes. Emma grated the homemade soap into small pieces when needed, and it would easily dissolve in the water.

The Ice Man

An iceman visited the Burkholders twice a week. He would come and replenish the ice in the icebox, which was like a refrigerator. Electric was in some surrounding areas, and this affected the iceman since one of the first appliances installed was usually an electric refrigerator. The iceman was very vocal in promoting the merits of using ice over electricity to keep food cool. The main thrust of his conversation was that the power company charged a minimum of $3.00 a month.

What a waste of hard-earned money!

John Burkholder's 8-16 International Tractor

About 1916, John Burkholder purchased an 8-16 International tractor. It received its name by its horsepower ratings. The tractor had sixteen horsepower on the belt and eight horsepower at the wheels. It was powered by an in-line four-cylinder engine, which was connected to a three-speed transmission. The steel wheels were driven by large chains, which transferred the power from the transmission. The tractor had a futuristic appearance with a steep forward-sloping hood. This was accomplished by placing the radiator at the rear of the engine, directly in front of the operator.

In the early 1930s, a windstorm swept through the valley. Numerous roofs lost their tin, including Michael's straw shed. Michael and the boys gathered all the scattered tin and placed it on a neat pile. John Burkholder's farm had an old quarry hole used as a dump, so Michael got permission to place the junk tin in the hole. This was before Michael had a tractor.

The tin dragged over the ground would have made a horrendous noise, alarming the horses, Bert and Pet; so Michael decided to use his father's 8-16 tractor to drag the tin to the old quarry hole. He wrapped a chain around the tin and drug it with his father's tractor out onto Route 73, across the concrete bridge, much to the delight of all the neighborhood boys.

Emma's Garden

Emma had her garden in the front of the house between the porch and Route 73, in plain view of all the neighborhood women as they went to church. Emma took special efforts to keep her garden orderly and weed- free.

One summer in the early 1930s, the state decided to pave Route 73. Up until this time, it had been a dirt road. They filled in the road right in front of Michael's farmstead creating an abundance of noise and dirt. The dust covered all of Emma's garden plants, plus she was embarrassed to work in the garden with all the strange men working on the road. Apparently, she complained to Michael because he remarked, " You might as well accept that there will be no evidence of pride in your garden this summer."

The little family grew as baby boys were added to the home. Titus, Weaver, John, Leon, and Frank, were added to the growing family. In those days, the doctor came to the home, sometimes spending the night to assist with the blessed event as children were added to the home. When Leon was born, Grandma Susan, who lived across the road, within easy viewing distance, noticed Doctor Wenger's car, and presumed why he had been called.

The next morning the Burkholder boys walked out the lane and headed for school. At the end of the lane, they joined their cousins, Daniel and John, who lived over on the farm at Trupe's Mill. As they walked up Route 625 towards school, they passed their Grandma Burkholder's house. She came out on the porch and asked, "Does the new baby have a name?"

"Leon," came the reply.

"Leon" responded Susan quickly, "What for name is that? That is a mule's name."

Daniel, noted for his quick wit retorted to his Grandmother Sus as she was commonly known, "Sus isn't a name I would write home about either."

The subject was quickly ended as Susan retreated into her house.

An 8-16 International Tractor like John Burkholder's.
Credit: *100 Years of Camera Scenes.*

With eight boys in the family, before Edna and Arlene were born, Michael had plenty of help. However, boys can also work in the house. Michael and Emma's boys had no qualms about working in the house. When Leon was asked to hang up the wash, he did it willingly, but kept a close watch on the road. Emma had a pulley line from a post just off the porch out to a pole along Route 73. Whenever a car came, he retreated into the house until it was past. The boys did their chores willingly, but maybe a bit more efficiently than their Mother knew about, especially when she wasn't around. When Titus and Lloyd were told to wash up the kitchen floor they found it much faster to use the garden hose, and then sweep the excess water to a convenient hole at the end of the kitchen.

Then there was the time that Frank was washing clothes in the old Maytag wringer washer. Somehow, he ran Michael's overalls through the wringer wrong, and they wrapped around the wringers and mutilated them. Emma was called to the disaster scene, but it was too late to salvage anything. She could not back the overalls out, by reversing the wringers, and finally she went and cut the overalls out with scissors. Frank fully expected to be punished by Michael for ruining his overalls. However, Emma took care of her little helper. She somehow produced another pair of overalls. Michael never missed the overalls, or found out about Frank's accident.

There is another incident where Emma sided with her helpers when Lizzie Wenger was visiting. She was an older lady, slightly deaf from scarlet fever in her youth, thus she had the habit of speaking quite loud. Lizzie, a high-energy person, was helping Emma with her sewing. She was operating the sewing machine at maximum speed, but her continuous chatter over-powered the sewing machine, both in volume and in momentum.

Leon, playing on the floor found it quite wearisome, so he quietly went into the basement and flipped the breaker, which supplied electricity to the sewing machine. Upstairs the high-speed hum ground to a halt, and momentarily its competition was also silent. When Leon came up the cellar steps into the kitchen, he fully expected a reprimand. However, Emma did not ask what he was doing, but silently ignored Leon. After Lizzie left, Leon made another trip to the cellar and the sewing machine worked fine again.

Tilling The Soil

In 1939, Michael purchased his first tractor—a Farmall, Model A. He paid $675 for the tractor, including a one-bottom, thirteen-inch plow, and a grass mower.

On June 1, 1944, Michael, gave the boys instructions to pull tobacco plants to transplant in the field in the afternoon. The boys spent the morning pulling tobacco seedlings out of the beds to replant in the field. Tobacco plants were set in the field by a person seated on the back of the planter, riding low to the ground with his feet sticking under a water tank. This person placed a seedling in a small pool of water, which was released from a tank on the planter. The planter mechanism that released the shot of water gave a sharp snap signaling the boys to set the plant. The planter water tank had to be refilled with water at the end of each round. They pumped the water from a supply tank set on a wagon placed on the field lane for this purpose.

"Raymond and Lloyd, go fill the water tank down in the Conestoga Creek," said Michael as soon the plants were pulled from the tobacco beds. The boys obediently hitched Pet and Bert to the wagon to pull the supply tank. The mules pulled the wagon into the Conestoga until they almost completely submerged the wagon. Taking five-gallon buckets, Raymond and Lloyd briskly dipped water out of the Conestoga, one on each side of the wagon, and poured it into the water supply tank as the mules patiently waited.

"Giddap!" exclaimed Lloyd, when the tank was full. Both mules pulled, seesawing back and forth, but the loaded wagon would not budge. "Whoa," Lloyd said reassuringly, and the mules settled down. However, Bert and Pet, knowing what was expected of them, no longer stood in relaxed patience. They pranced about with their ears standing straight up, making little lunges into their harness, in anticipation of the order they knew would come. Lloyd was standing on the wagon in a stoop forward position, holding the reins tightly. He watched the mules closely to see when they were in the proper position to give them the command to pull.

Lloyd waited until both mules were stepping back in their harnesses simultaneously, snapped the reins and yelled 'Giddap!" Both mules lunged forward together, hunkered down, putting their cooperative efforts into pulling the heavily-loaded wagon out of the Conestoga Creek.

Lloyd relaxed slightly, as he felt the wagon beginning to move under him, but suddenly a loud crack startled him. The wagon broke and the mules pulled the front wheels from under the wagon bed. Lloyd still holding the reins tightly was suddenly yanked head-first into the Conestoga Creek. Lloyd, still holding the reins, floundered through the water. As he was dragged up the muddy stream bank, Raymond, standing on the wagon bed, scrambled for the shore as the loaded wagons' front portion settled on the Conestoga streambed. As Raymond scrambled up the creek bank, he heard Lloyd coughing and spluttering and finally a shout "Whoa, Whoa!" Bert and Pet stopped stamping their feet impatiently. Finally, Lloyd, a bedraggled and muddied sight, struggled to his feet. Lloyd slowly limped back to the creek. "I guess tobacco planting will be delayed today," exclaimed Raymond as they stood on the stream bank looking at the sorry situation.

The boys headed to tell Michael of the collapsed wagon in the middle of the creek. Michael came, surveyed the situation, and told the boys to drain the tank, as much as they could with it being partly submerged. In the meantime, he went for a tractor and a chain. They pulled the wagon and empty tank out on the creek bank and saw that the reach pole had snapped. The boys jacked the front of the wagon up while Michael made a new reach pole.

By three o'clock in the afternoon, the repaired wagon, full of water and loaded with boxes of tobacco seedlings to transplant, was pulled to the tobacco field. Bert and Pet were stepping lively with Michael urging them along. The snap of the water release went considerably faster than usual that afternoon. Raymond and Lloyd's hands flew setting seedlings, and before dark, all the tobacco plants were planted in nice straight rows.

Scarlet Fever in the Valley

Before the days of advanced medical knowledge, it was common for a disease to sweep through the Weaverland Valley causing much suffering and death. When these epidemics were raging, funerals were sometimes sparsely attended, for fear of catching the dreaded diseases. During an epidemic during World War I, numerous deaths in Lancaster County caused a serious shortage of caskets. The local manufacturers could not keep up with the demand. Conestoga Traction Company dispatched a freight trolley to Boyertown on a sixty-mile emergency run. The trolley returned with a full load of caskets desperately needed by Lancaster County morticians.

In the mid-1930s, scarlet fever was ravaging the valley. When a family had scarlet fever, the Public Health Service quarantined the family, so that no physical contact could be made with them. They would place a large sign on the house doors, warning that the family had a contagious disease. No family member was supposed to leave the premises, neither was anyone to come to the premises. When a family was quarantined, no one was allowed to attend school, placing a burden on the students because on return they were behind. Groceries were brought by the neighbors and placed on the porch of the quarantined family. In those days, the doctor made house calls instead of asking the patient to go to his office.

The Michael Burkholder family was quarantined as most of the family had a touch of the dreaded scarlet fever. John and Weaver were very sick and Dr. Wenger came twice a week to check on the sick boys. Even though the family was quarantined, grandfather John W. Burkholder came to visit his sick grandchildren. The next time that Grandpa John went to Trupe's Mill to sit a while for a social visit with the other local farmers, they admonished him. They chastened him about his unconcern for the rest of the community in exposure to the disease and visiting a public place. Even the road walkers (bums) turned around and left when they saw the dreaded notices hanging on the doors of those who were quarantined. After the family had recuperated, Dr. Wenger confided in Michael that he had feared for John and Weaver's lives at the worst of the disease, but both survived with no after effects.

After the worst of the disease was over and the quarantine had been lifted, Titus was still sick in bed with the scarlet fever. Michael and Emma and most of the children went to church one Sunday while Raymond and Melvin stayed home with Titus. After an hour or so when the time began to drag, Raymond suggested that petting their pony, Topsy, would cheer Titus. Melvin agreed and both boys went out to the barn to get Topsy. Placing the halter on Topsy, they led her to the front porch. Topsy balked, so Melvin went into the house to get some pretzels. Well, Topsy also went through the front door of the house, around the kitchen table, trotted up and around the circular steps going upstairs with no more concern than if he was going to the feed trough. The steps creaked in protest as they ascended to the upstairs bedroom. The willing pony trotted right into the bedroom where Titus was recuperating. Titus naturally perked up as he petted Topsy. (Whether it was from the added attention, the spectacle of a pony in his upstairs bedroom, or the anticipation of how Raymond and Melvin were going to get Topsy downstairs again, is not remembered.)

After spending some time with Titus, the boys decided it was time to take the pony to the barn again. However, going down the steps was altogether different from coming up. Topsy balked at the top of the steps. After much coaxing and pulling, he made a gigantic leap and in two leaps, the pony was back down in Emma's clean kitchen, sliding across her clean linoleum floor. Topsy regained her footing and Raymond and Lloyd calmly led Topsy around the kitchen table and out the front door, to the barn.

The year 1936 was a trying year for the Burkholder family. Emma was very sick for a large portion of the year. Leon was the baby and he was at Daniel Hoover's a large portion of the year. For three months, Dr. Wenger from Terre Hill visited the Burkholder residence every day. During some of the worst days, the doctor came twice a day.

Years later, in the mid 1950s, an interesting artifact became known. There was a dump on the John Burkholder farm, by then owned by Isaac Hurst. Their children were scrounging in the dump and came across some of Dr. Wenger's old ledger books. Apparently, he was cleaning house and discarded some of his early ledger books at the dump. The 1936 ledger book recorded all of his daily visits, as well as the birth of a new baby which Michael and Emma named Frank. All these visits were carried on the book, billed, and paid at the end of the year for a grand total of $80.

Bill's Bold Bolt

One of Michael's boys usually went over to Susan's house on Sunday mornings to get her horse and buggy hitched, and ready for church. One Sunday morning, Raymond had been over, placed the harness on Susan's horse, Bill, hitched him to the buggy and had the rig all ready for Susan to attend church. Raymond had no more than returned home when Susan came on her front porch and hollered to Michael that Isaac Hurst's family was picking her up to go along to church. Bill had been hitched up and eagerly waiting to get some exercise, as he had been in the barn all week.

Until Raymond returned to Susan's place to unhitch Bill and the buggy, Susan had left for church and Michael and the rest of the family was gone. Bill was not anxious to be placed back in his barn, as he had not been exercised all week and was eager to go. Raymond decided to take him for a run. Taking Bill out on Route 73,[11] he turned right toward Spring Grove and Bill started to show his spirit. However, as Raymond approached the lane of his home he suddenly decided that Lloyd and Titus would also like to go along. Titus had injured his foot, and was not going to church, and Raymond and Lloyd were staying home with him. Bill already had his heart set to run, but responded willingly to Raymond's tug on the left rein at the last moment. Bill turned left into Michael's farm lane causing the buggy to fishtail its rear wheels as it came around the bend.

Lloyd came running with Titus hobbling behind when they saw Bill coming, not wanting to miss any excitement. Raymond coaxed Bill to a quick halt and they were off! Around the house and out the lower drive, Bill was anxious to go. Coming to the highway, Bill turned right, needing no guidance; he was headed for church. Turning right on Route 73, away they went, but right ahead was a long slow line of buggies, all families in their buggies plodding to church. Bill, with his spirits in high mettle was not to be held back, "maybe neither were the boys," because after a few half-hearted attempts to hold Bill's speed down, the reins went slack. The left lane was clear! At a full pounding gallop, Bill took the left lane. The boys hunched down in the buggy, striving not to be recognized. One by one as Bill's outstretched head would approach the rear of an overtaken buggy, its driver, alerted by the galloping horse and the rattle of the speeding buggy, would suddenly pop his head out the driver's door. Again and again, a face with a wide-eyed, open-mouthed expression, would appear, and beside him, his wife also leaning over and peering over his shoulder, would watch Bill, and Susan's buggy, race past at breakneck speed. With much coaxing, Raymond guided Bill to turn left at the next intersection, and away from the long line of buggies headed for church.

---

[11] Route 73 was changed to Route 625.

1933 Conestoga School. Front row, left to right: Raymond Hurst, Lester Stauffer, Martin Fenner, Alfred Troupe, Marlin Burkholder, Martin Weber, Earl Hurst, Melvin Burkholder, and Ammon Weaver. Second row: Melvin Stauffer, Mervin Heisy, David Hurst, Mary Martin, Clarence Good, Irene Martin, Raymond Weber, Lloyd Burkholder, Lester Martin, Paul Good, John Dan Burholder, and Raymond Burkholder (author's father). Third row: Minnie Martin, Ester Gehman, Emma Zimmerman, Martha Good, Elva Zimmerman, Emma Good, Ruth Troupe, Mabel Weber, Elizabeth Gehman, and Ida Weber. Fourth row: teacher Pearl Wallece, Nora Martin, Harry Stauffer, Harold Gehman, Harvey Zimmerman, and Mary Weaver.

There was more than the weather discussed before the church services that morning. One person was reported remarking, "Susan sure was in a hurry to get to church this morning." Susan sat calmly at her place in church, completely innocent and unaware of the commotion her horse had made that morning.

"Thrashing" Tales

The wives of the farmers where the threshing crew worked went to great lengths to preserve their reputation to set a good meal. Any woman who ran out of a certain food item was highly embarrassed and felt her reputation as a cook was tarnished.

In any thrashing crew, there were always a few pranksters. When threshing at Abram Zeisets, the pies must have been especially good, because they were all eaten! Harry Martin, noticing that the pie plates were all empty, made a special request. Naturally, he wanted another piece of pie, forcing the ladies to admit that there were no more available.

Several days later, it was time to thrash at Harry Martin's farm. The pranksters convinced the rest of the crew to go light on the main course of the noon meal, but then eat pie until it was all gone. The beginning of the meal went fine, with lots of food left. But when Mrs. Harry Martin served the pie, the first person tipped the pie alongside of his plate, and used his fork to slide half the pie onto his plate. As he passed the rest of the pie to his seatmate, he remarked, "This pie looks extra good." Sliding the rest of the pie on his plate, the seatmate replied, "I think so too." The rest of the threshing crew all had a mischievous grin on their faces as they watched the beginnings of the planned prank.

As Harry watched the second and third pie disappear in a like manner he turned to his wife and said, "More pie Mommy." His wife Elizabeth, turned and headed for the basement. In a moment, Elizabeth returned with her arms stretched in front of her, carrying a pie in each hand and balancing two more pies on each of her arms. Giving these six pies to the men at the table, Elizabeth, turned and went into the basement again and repeated the performance, also setting these on the table. As she surveyed the table filled with pies, a satisfied grin appeared on her face. The men ate a lot of pie, but they were denied the satisfaction of asking for pie and not receiving any. Elizabeth had gotten an inkling of her husband's episode at Abram Zeisets, and knowing human nature, spent a busy morning making sure that her reputation of setting an adequate table was not tarnished.

The New Engineer

Most threshing rigs, of days gone by, were powered by steam engines. These wheezing, puffing, chugging, smoke belching, yet powerful steam engines were considered a masterpiece of engineering in those days when horsepower was predominant. The steam engine was made of iron and steel, yet when fired, it seemed to come alive. It snorted, sighed, and seemed to breathe. Under a load, it hummed and roared purposely like a living thing. The operator of the steam engine, or the engineer, had an enviable position which most young men looked at with admiration. Many a person aspired to be the engineer, to fire and control this powerful mechanism.

However, with this position came responsibility. The steam engine was the heart of the threshing crew. It powered the threshing machine with a long belt. If not enough power was generated, the whole crew was slowed down. The ripe grain in the field, waiting to be threshed was at stake. The fruit of a whole year's work was brought to a finale. A steam engine used fire to heat water which produced steam. The steam drove a piston, turning the steam into mechanical energy. (If the fire was not tended properly, insufficient steam was generated to power the threshing machine.) There was a fine art to properly firing a steam engine, and not all could fully bring these smoke-belching iron beasts to their full potential.

The other side of the threshing crew was the horses and men, which fed wheat into the threshing machine to be threshed. The golden grain flowed into bags and the straw was blown on a dusty pile. If the threshers did not feed the threshing machine fast enough, a surplus of steam was produced. This steam has to be released, as it would produce excess pressure in the boiler and cause it to explode. Thus, steam engines had a safety device. When the pressure in the boiler reached a certain level, it released some of the steam into the atmosphere with a marvelous roar, which could be heard all over the neighborhood.

The threshing crews of the Weaverland Valley usually consisted of younger men who enjoyed nothing more than a little competition. While they worked together in perfect harmony, like a well-engineered machine, there was always a spirit of competition among them.

The drivers of the wagon teams bringing the wheat from the field strived to get to the threshing machine before the wagon in front of them was unloaded. This gave them the opportunity to enlighten the team unloading in front of them about the finer points of pitching sheaves.

Nevertheless, at the first inkling of inadequate power from the steam engine, the whole threshing crew was brought together into a united frenzy of effort to run the engine out of steam. If they could accomplish this, they would have time to take a break while the engineer gave the steam engine time to catch up and rebuild steam pressure. Not only could the men take a break, but they also gather around the steam engine and give the engineer some direct and pointed advice on his ability to fire the steam engine.

One fine July day this is exactly what was happening. As the young men with wagons in the field picked up sheaves, they tried to outdo each other in the time it took to gather a load. The pace was hectic under the hot summer sun and the dust rose under the pounding horse's feet as they brought load after load of sheaves to the threshing machine to be thrashed. The dusty men, hot and sweaty, pitched the sheaves on their wagon in record time and welcomed the short break as the horses pulled the loaded wagon to the thresher. However, the short interlude did not keep the drivers from urging their horses into a gallop. Arriving at the threshing machine, a blizzard of sheaves was thrown on the table keeping the threshing machine running at full capacity. Eventually the threshing machine began to slow down from lack of power from the steam engine. Finally, the foreman gave the engineer a signal to blow the whistle, telling the crew to discontinue feeding the threshing machine, letting it clean out and then stop. The grain stopped flowing, the straw ceased to be blown on the straw pile, and gradually the dust settled. Not enough steam was being produced and the steam engine needed time to build up steam pressure again. This was the third time the crew had brought the work to a halt because of lack of sufficient steam.

The crew was relentlessly hounding the engineer when a quiet young man asked the foreman for the opportunity to fire the steam engine. The foreman had noticed that this young man had been taking a keen interest in the workings of the steam engine, asking many questions and offering to help in lubricating and starting it up. Figuring this young aspiring engineer could do no worse than the engineer that was presently firing the engine, he gave the necessary orders, and the crew had a new engineer. All kinds of predictions of the length of time needed to deplete the steam with this new engineer at the controls were brought forth. However, this young engineer, paid no heed. He was busy building a thin even fire in the firebox, preheating the water in the water heater before introducing it to the boiler, and checking the try cocks and water gauge to see if the proper level of water was in the boiler. He knew that once the steam pressure was built to 160 pounds, and the power was again applied to the threshing machine that he was going to be put to the test. A glance over the boiler and out the long, now motionless belt connecting to the threshing machine showed a long line of waiting teams and wagons loaded with wheat sheaves, to be unloaded and threshed. He wanted everything to be in order before the test. The crew was going to be relentless to bring this newly-aspired engineer, a position many of them secretly sought, to naught, and bring the steam engine, his responsibility, to a halt.

When the steam pressure was back up to 160 pounds, the foreman tooted the whistle, ordering the crew back to work. The young engineer slowly engaged the clutch carefully bringing the threshing machine up to speed. Adjusting the governor to a steady 250-RPM, he turned his attention back to the firebox. As the crew started to throw sheaves on the threshing table to be fed into the threshing machine, he started the "blower." Injecting steam through a vent in the stack, which through the venturi principle, sucked air through the firebox, forced the fire into a glowing blowtorch. It also blew all the accumulated soot right out the stack in an evil cloud of black smoke, but it produced heat, which produced steam.

The contest was on! The threshing crew, a whole herd of horses and wagons, a whole field of ripe golden grain, and the threshing machine against a lone engineer and a steam engine connected by the long whirring, dancing belt racing back and forth from the engine to threshing machine. As the crew fed the thrashing machine sheaves, and a load was applied, the continuous belt ran straight and true on the pulled or powered side. Whispering little ripples started to appear on the slack or returning side.

The new engineer was too busy to notice this. He was busy watching the water level, adding water as the boiler heated the water to steam, yet being careful not to add too much at one time and chill the water in the boiler. He was quickly opening the fire door stoking the fire with swift small scoops of coal to the spots burning thin on the fire bed.

He kept the fire thin and even, making sure there were no thick spots, which restricted airflow, and no thin spots which would not produce heat. Occupied by controlling the airflow to the firebox to keep the fire burning at peak capacity, he noticed the team of horses trying to sneak around the back of the steam engine. The driver was striving to get a peek at the engines' steam pressure gauge. With detached nonchalance, the engineer busied himself wiping the dust on the pressure gauge as the inquisitive team driver hustled past, thus depriving him of what he wanted to know.

After a couple minutes, the engineer noticed the steam engine was running slightly over the recommended 250 Rpm. He adjusted the governor accordingly, causing a slight slowdown in the threshing machine. The threshing crew noticed this slight slow down, grinned and nodded their head to each other, and redoubled their efforts in anticipation of a break on account of lack of sufficient steam.

Under the careful control of the new engineer, the steam engine hummed and roared purposely like a living thing. Each time the slide valve opened giving the piston a shot of steam a hollow pulsating thump was heard. The governor continued to spin merrily on top of the engine among wisps of escaping steam. The stack belched a continuous stream of black smoke, fringed with white, from spent steam used to power the "blower." The huge flywheel continued relentlessly on, spinning rapidly, it spokes a blur, pulling the endless belt, which powered the threshing machine

Suddenly this organized frenzy of activity was shattered by a piercing blast. The safety valve was blowing off excess steam! Despite the threshing crews' best efforts under the new engineer's command, the steam engine was producing all the power that was needed and even had steam to spare. With a jubilant grin, the new engineer gave a loud long blast on the engine's whistle, signaling mastery to the whole crew. The rest of the crew at the threshing machine and those in the field gathering sheaves, hearing the roar of excess released steam, and then the long blast on the whistle, had to acknowledge defeat. With a new engineer, the engine had steam to spare. Work continued at a normal pace and they took their break at lunch.

Boyhood Nonsense

One brisk fall morning, Michael gave his two eldest sons the chore of harvesting the potatoes, and storing them in the cold cellar. Michael had dug the potatoes with Bert and a potato plow. The boys hitched Bert to the wagon, gathered some bushel baskets, and headed for the potato patch. Melvin guided Bert to a stop alongside the rows of the dug potatoes. The two boys each took a row gathering the potatoes into their bushel baskets, and when they were full, dumped them into the wagon. As the boys moved down their rows, the wagon was left behind, and one of them would yell "Giddap Bert" and Bert would move forward until someone would command him to stop with a "Whoa Bert."

All went well for a while, but Melvin started to move ahead of Raymond. Instead of putting forth effort to catch up to Melvin, Raymond continued working at a relaxed pace, and Melvin's lead lengthened. Melvin would command Bert to move ahead, and not wanting to carry his potatoes any further than necessary, Raymond would almost immediately yell for Bert to stop. Raymond was not willing to step up his pace and Melvin likewise did not deem it necessary to help his brother. After a time of this foolishness, Bert started showing his agitation, standing with her ears standing straight up nervously flicking her tail. The boys, mindful only of their own controversy, paid Bert no attention.

"Giddap" yelled Melvin and Bert ambled forward obediently. Almost instantly came the command from Raymond, "Whoa." However, Bert having had enough of this foolishness had another idea. At the command of "Whoa," instead of stopping, she threw her head in the air and with a mighty "hee-haw," increased her pace to a trot. Making a hard left-hand u-turn, scraping the steering wheels against the wagon box, she headed for the barn. Both boys tried to grab Bert's harness as she galloped past, but Bert neatly sidestepped them and was gone.

Melvin and Raymond headed for the barn, not too pleased at the prospect of the walk and the possibility of an explanation why Bert was at the barn. Their worst fears were fulfilled as they came to the last turn before the farmstead. Bert apparently had cut the corner short and the wagon had run over several rows of corn. Michael, who was standing at the corner surveying the flattened corn, asked the boys. "What happened?"

"Bert ran away" was the humble reply.

"Bert ran away, nothing doing. Bert has never run away before. What happened?" After some probing questions, the story came out. Following some fatherly admonitions, the boys went to the barn, got Bert again, and returned to the potato patch.

A Change of Heart

Jacob Horst's farm was situated directly across the Conestoga Creek from Michael Burkholder's farm. Each farm has a direct view of the other. At times, all work ceased on the Horst farm to observe the antics taking place on the Burkholder farm.

In one instance, two of Michael's boys were returning from an errand with the two mules, Bert and Pet. They pulled the mule and spring wagon under the forebay in the front of the barn. All went fine as they unhitched Bert and Pet and led them into their stalls in the barn. The two boys returned to the spring wagon and prepared to push it into the carriage shed. At the entrance of the carriage shed was a slight ledge. As the front of the wagon wheel approached this ledge, pulled by Lloyd at the shaft and pushed by Raymond at the rear, Raymond stopped pushing the wagon. Lloyd at the front gave an extra pull to get the wagon up over the ledge. However, his efforts alone were not enough and the wagon snapped to a stop.

Both boys backed the spring wagon back further, to get a good run and try again.

On the second try, the spring wagon had sufficient speed to roll in the shed. Just before the front wheel reached the ledge, Raymond grabbed

• 53 •

the spokes of the rear wheel, and held it from going around, causing the wagon to again roll up to the ledge and stop. By now David Horst, from his site across the creek was watching these developments with interest. However, Lloyd also had a clue that there was something amiss.

Both boys pulled the wagon back again, got a good run, but just as the front wheels reached the ledge Lloyd stopped pulling, whirled around, just as Raymond grasped the wagon wheel, causing it to drag on the stones. Lloyd dropped the shafts and raced toward Raymond with intents only known in boyhood wisdom of yonder years. However, Raymond, understanding those intents, and with boyhood foresight, was already fleeing the scene of the impending calamity.

David watched with a big grin on his face, as the two boys raced out of the front and then along the side of barn. As the boys disappeared, out of David's sight, behind the barn, he wondered what the outcome would be. But almost instantly, before he could even turn back to his work, wonders of all wonders, Lloyd and Raymond again appeared, walking peaceably side by side, seeming without a care in the world. They moseyed back, retraced the same path they had furiously scrambled only seconds before, with seeming, completely different intents. A moment later Michael also appeared, following the boys. Lloyd and Raymond came back to the spring wagon and each took their former positions. The wagon glided into the shed as slick as a whistle, but under the careful scrutiny of Michael standing at the corner of the barn.

Cleaning Out the Stables

Every Saturday morning it was the boys' job to clean out the horse stables. All the soiled straw was removed and replaced with clean and fresh straw. However, since the straw was only partly soiled, it was not removed to the manure pile. It was taken to the steer pen to make full use of its absorbing properties. Boys being boys, they were always looking for a quicker and easier way to do their chores. Melvin and Raymond were given this chore one Saturday morning. Instead of making the numerous trips to the steer stable with a wheelbarrow as they usually did, they decided to use the manure sled. It was a simple platform with runners underneath to which a horse or mule was hooked to pull it.

The boys pulled the manure sled to the stables and forked the week's accumulation on the sled. As they were hooking Bert to the sled to pull it over to the steer pen, they were congratulating themselves on how easy this chore was compared to using the wheelbarrow. Melvin took the reins and gave Bert the command "Giddap." Out the stable door came the load of manure, with Raymond running ahead to open the steer stable pen. The sled pulled easily and Bert pranced through the steer stable door. However, the manure sled was wider than the door and it came to sudden stop. Bert feeling the load increase did as all good mules do. He hunched down and pulled harder, and before Melvin could say "Whoa," the harness tore, yanking Melvin off the top of the load into the steer stable. Melvin and Raymond surveyed the scene. The job was still not done and the wheelbarrow was then called back to its duty hauling the straw the rest of the way into the steer stable.

• Chapter Eight •

Automobiles and the Mennonites

In 1927, the Weaverland Mennonite Church was in turmoil because of the car issue. Michael and Emma decided to purchase a car. Michael went to Terre Hill and purchased a 1927 Chevrolet from the AG Oberholtzer Chevrolet dealership operated by Pit & Arch Oberholtzer. The car was dark blue with black fenders and had a ragtop. It had wooden spoke wheels with pinstripes and a big spare tire on the back of the car. The windows were semi-transparent curtains which were snapped on in the winter and removed in the summer. These cars, known as Touring Cars were four-door convertibles with a ragtop, but the Mennonites never "smashed the top" or folded the top back as most car owners did in the summer. Touring cars were the only affordable cars available at this time. Only the luxury cars were fully enclosed.

However, after he had purchased the car, but before the car was delivered, Michael perceived that if he would wait a bit he could avoid the stigma associated with having a car before the church officially approved it. The church, at that point, had not yet approved of their members having a car. He placed his car in storage at the dealership and waited until the Wenger and Horning groups split, and then went with the Horning group.

Michael's uncle, David W. Burkholder, was involved with an intriguing plan in hope of preventing the 1927 church split. One of the contentions against the car was that they involved pride. The shiny paint and chrome was regarded as worldly and an affront to Christian humility. David W. Burkholder is remembered as saying, "I recognize the convenience of a car, and if I could have a car I would not wash it as a sign of lack of pride." Another idea considered was a plan to remove the big chrome headlights from the front of the car during day-time use.

David W. Burkholder, Henry B. Hoover, and Daniel Good, went with Deacon Martin Zimmerman on a quest to find a plain and suitable car to solve the perplexing problem. They went to York, Pennsylvania, and visited the Durant automobile manufacturing plant. Deacon Martin Zimmerman special-ordered a car, manufactured to their specifications, which they hoped, would be acceptable to those opposed to the fancy automobiles. This special-built car, with plain contour, and lack of ornaments was built and delivered to Martin's home in Ephrata. The rear of the car lacked the curved storage enclosure for the folding top. There was simply a flat panel at the rear of the car. Since the Mennonites never took the top down, there was no need for it. The front of the car was also modified. On top of the windshield, there was a protruding square lip. This style was copied from the buggies, and this style of construction can still be seen on the buggies today.

However, the cost of special-building a car was prohibitive, and Martin Zimmerman's plan never materialized. He placed his car into storage, not using it until the church officially approved them at the 1927 spring conference. Then he used this car as his personal car. However, the concept of a plain and boxy contour familiar to a buggy, and special-ordered in Martin Zimmerman's Durant was recognized and maintained. The early touring cars had elaborately upholstered rear seats that were easily visible to all pedestrians. This was a stumbling block to the otherwise old-fashioned appearance and out-dated style of the touring cars. When the car was accepted by church leaders, this was to be rectified by placing an extra canvas from the back door around the back of the car to the back door on the other side of the car—effectively giving the car a boxy appearance and hiding the rear seat. This was accepted and practiced by the ministry and the conservative element of the Old Order Mennonites, but this issue soon became irrelevant. Used touring cars soon became scarce and difficult to purchase.

The car manufacturers were introducing sedans or closed cars at a more affordable price range. The Old Order Mennonites did not purchase them as they considered them to be modern and worldly.

A picture of the plain Durant automobile purchased by Deacon Martin Zimmerman in an effort to find a practical solution in hopes to avoid a car-buggy division.

About 1935, however, the touring cars were becoming very difficult to obtain, and the church leaders were in a quandary.

A special meeting was held on July 5, 1935, and most of the Old Order church leaders were in favor of allowing the sedans, but one deacon was opposed to these fully-enclosed automobiles, feeling they promoted pride. Finally, Martin Zimmerman proposed a compromise that would allow the use of sedans, but require the cars to be totally black, including all the chrome. This was accepted and this was the beginning of the "Black Bumpers" nickname, which is still prevalent today.

When the transition was made from touring cars to allowing sedans, a car dealership in New Holland was also affected. This dealership courted the Mennonite trade and kept his eyes open for good used touring cars, because he knew he had a ready market for them.

When the conference allowed the sedan, this dealership suddenly had many touring cars made available to him. The day after conference, this dealership purchased four touring cars to resell. However, he soon found out that his market for these cars had suddenly dried up, and he was stuck with them.

Antifreeze was very expensive and most people drained the water from their engines when cold weather came. Every time they wanted to use the car, they would fill the radiator with water and drain it when they arrived home again.

Michael stored his 1927 Chevrolet in a shed some distance from the barn. Wanting to use his car, he started it and drove it from the shed to the barn to fill the radiator with water. Letting the car run, he filled a bucket with water and poured it in the radiator. However, the cold water and the warm engine resulted in a cracked engine head. The proposed outing was delayed and replaced by a long wait for repair parts and a large bill. From then on, the water was carried to the car shed and the radiator was filled before the engine was started.

Shortly after Michael purchased his car, his father-in-law, Frank Weaver purchased a Ford Model A. Michael and Emma, with their young boys, and Frank and his wife decided to go in Frank's new Ford Model A to view the Conowingo Dam which was being constructed on the Susquehanna River in lower Lancaster County. Raymond as a five-year-old boy recalls Michael driving and when they came to a smooth stretch of road, Frank remarked in Pennsylvania Dutch, "If you are so minded, you can let her out. "Letting her out" refers to letting the horses reins hang loose and letting her run at top speed. Therefore, Michael let the Model A out. Top speed of a Model A, down a hard hill was about 70, so on level ground with two families along, "letting her out"' was not as dangerous as it would be with the automobiles today.

The Old Model T Ford

Abraham Horst had an old Ford Model T used as a runaround on the farm. It had no body anymore, just the frame, hood, and seats. No tires were on the wheels. The car was driven on its spoke-wheeled rims. However, the motor ran and the wheels went around. This was sufficient mechanized mobilization to naturally attract the young boys on a Sunday afternoon when they gathered. Young boys then apparently were no different then than they are today.

• 59 •

Father Abraham recognized this attraction and hid the crank. In the days before self-starters, the only way to start an automobile was to crank the engine until it started. At least so most people thought. On this fine afternoon, a group of boys was gathered around this dilapidated old Model T Ford. It was a great temptation with the potential of great fun, but with no crank. There was no way to start the engine. They could not push the car, as the tireless rims would just slide as soon as the clutch was engaged. However, necessity works wonders.

One of the boys came up with a splendid idea—at least in the minds of the boys. Moses, a son of Abraham Horst, jacked up the Model T, took a long rope, and wrapped it around the rear wheel. All the boys grabbed hold of the rope and pulled. Using the wheel like a recoil starter, with a mighty united tug on the rope, they managed to get the engine running. Removing the jack and letting the Model T down on its wheels again, they were ready for an afternoon of fun racing over the farm grounds, even though its crank was nowhere to be found.

Not all the drivers were experienced with the unusual controls of the Model T.

The Model T had three pedals on the floorboard; one was pressed to go forward, one for reverse, and one for the brakes. The boys were racing up to the corn fodder stack and at the last instant, stomped on the reverse pedal, seeing how close they could come to the corn fodder stack before the Model T came to a stop and backed up. Finally, as can be expected, one of the boys miscalculated, panicked, and pushed the wrong pedal ramming the Model T into the corn fodder stack. Amidst the cloud of dust, the hidden motor roared as the rear wheels spun furiously forward, then suddenly changed directions. The disturbed stack of loose corn fodder descended gracefully, covering all but the rear-end of the dilapidated car chassis. Nevertheless, the wheels continued spinning and eventually a dirty, dusty, and coughing driver emerged from under the corn fodder stack still sitting on the dilapidated Model T.

• *Chapter Nine* •

Conestoga Traction Company

In the early 1900s, another mode of transportation was made available to the community. The Conestoga Traction Company had a trolley line, originating in Lancaster, which came through the Weaverland Valley. It followed today's Route 23 traveling through Bareville, Groffdale, New Holland, and Blue Ball. From Blue Ball it crossed the Conestoga River near today's Martin's Limestone and ended in Terre Hill. A person could purchase a round-trip trolley ticket at Terre Hill and travel to Lancaster and return for 78 cents. The trolleys departed about every hour starting about 5:00 a.m. in the morning and traveled until midnight.

Conestoga Traction Company had lines radiating out from Lancaster to all portions of Lancaster County. By traveling to Lancaster, a person could connect to trolleys or trains traveling to Philadelphia, Harrisburg, Reading, or Baltimore.

This form of transportation began in 1874 in the city of Lancaster, using horse-drawn trolley cars. Horses were used until 1890 when the trolley lines were electrified. The trolley cars received their electric power from overhead electric lines. During these years there were many small routes operating under many companies. In 1899, the Conestoga Traction Company was formed which consolidated all these lines into one organized and efficient company. They started construction on routes to many outlying communities. New Holland received trolley service in January 1901.

In 1904, the New Holland line was extended to Blue Ball and Terre Hill. By the close of 1904 the Conestoga Traction Company, with the city

• 61 •

A Conestoga Traction Company trolley car is shown going west on Main in New Holland about 1905. To the right is the old Styer Building now replaced by a modern store owned by Nathan Rubinson, called Rubinson's Department Store. The building to the right behind the trolley car is a general store owned by Eli Hess. Note the cobblestone street. (On June 21, 1901, The Conestoga Traction Company ran its first passenger cars into the western end of New Holland. The tracks stopped at the location shown in the above photo. According to information from some older residents, the trolley car did not run through the length of New Holland until July 15, 1903.)

of Lancaster as its hub, had trolley tracks radiating in all directions, forming a transportation system covering most of Lancaster County.

The line was not only used by passengers. Freight business was also lucrative.

Farmers hauled their milk to the stops and the express cars would deliver it to the creamery in Lancaster. The Ephrata Route had a lucrative milk-hauling contract with Hershey Chocolate which connected to the Lebanon trolley system at Schafferstown. The farmers would deliver their milk cans to the trolley stops and place them on elevated platforms flush with the trolley floor. The trolley would silently glide in and stop. The door would open and the full cans would be slid into the trolley and the empty cans from the day before would be slid out on the platform. In moments, the trolley would be on its way to the next stop. The trolleys also delivered the mail and all types of agricultural articles.

Lancaster County tourism roots are ascribed to the trolley system. In the early 1900s, the magazine *Pennsylvania German* ran a series of articles describing picturesque trolley travel. The Conestoga Traction Company reprinted and distributed these articles in booklet form. The booklet, *Seeing Lancaster County from a Trolley Window*, soon became an essential guide to touring the Amish countryside in the pre-automobile days.

Nevertheless, the automobile made gradual inroads on the trolley service. By 1930, riders and freight were down and the Conestoga Traction Company was losing money. It started to close down some of it lines. Trolley service to Blue Ball and Terre Hill was discontinued in 1932.

World War II rejuvenated the trolley line. As gas rationing came into effect and tires became unavailable, the community returned to the

---

Left, bottom: One of the express cars of The Conestoga Traction Company in 1909 on Main Street in New Holland used to carry mail and freight to merchants and farmers throughout the county. These cars put the stagecoach and the Conestoga wagon out of business because is was faster and more reliable in bad weather. On January 25, 1909, the Conestoga Traction Company began carrying mail to Earl and East Earl Townships; before then, mail was carried by stage coaches several times a week, while the Conestoga wagon served the farms and merchants.

Terre Hill Terminal Shed used by passengers and freight customers.

trolley system for their travel needs. However, it was short-lived. After the war, the people returned to their automobiles. On September 21, 1947, trolley service in Lancaster County ceased. However, while it was in service, many people used the trolley service for a trip to the big city of Lancaster for their business needs. A popular outing for a group of girls was taking the trolley on a shopping trip to Lancaster City. It is rumored that Michael, as a young man, wanted to impress his special friend, and they took the trolley to Lancaster on a special outing. Michael's brother-in-law, Amos "Sonny" Hurst, was employed as a conductor for Conestoga Traction Company on a city route when he was a young man.

It surely was a pleasant way to travel. Almost silently, the electric-powered trolley car glided along, not too fast, but still much faster than a trotting horse as the country scenery passed by the open window. When one of the other trolleys climbed the hill at the Blue Ball hill, the rest of the trolleys on the line almost came to a stop, because the hill-climbing trolley required all the power in the overhead electric line.

◆ Chapter Ten ◆

Trupe's Mill Experiences

The interior of Trupe's Mill was not only an attraction for the neighborhood, it also attracted all kinds of vermin. All kinds of insects were drawn to the grain. Rats and mice were also drawn to the abundant food supply. The bounteous bags of feed and grain gave ample hiding places for them to seek protection. "Carbysulfate," a gas product, was frequently used to rid the mill of these pests. The downside of this product was that it was highly explosive.

When the mill was shut down in the evening, Carbysulfate was released starting on the top floor of the mill. Scampering down to the next floor, more was released until the whole mill was saturated with this gas. Samuel Trupe, Jr., remarked, "When you reached the bottom of the mill, it was high time to get out yourself."

Once, Clarence Martin, an employee of the mill used a match for light when he was checking the interior of a feed storage bin in the upper story of the mill. He did not realize that Samuel Trupe had treated the grain a short time before. The explosion blew his cap off, and started the dust on the rafters on fire. Luckily, Clarence managed to get the fire out before it spread.

In a different instance, Alfred Trupe, a son of Samuel Trupe, and Melvin Burkholder were unloading grain from a truck and storing it in the mill. They were using the outside hoist. Alfred told Melvin to take four 100-pound bags at a time instead of the usual three. Melvin obeyed and wrapped the chain around four bags. Alfred standing at the receiving door high above pulled the hoist control rope and nothing happened. "Just wait a minute," called Alfred, as he disappeared. Alfred ran to the top of the mill and applied some sticky tacky belt dressing to the belt, which operated the hoist. In a moment he was back down at the door and again he pulled the hoist control rope. The four bags rose majestically from the truck. The bags rose to the open door where Alfred was waiting to receive them. When they reached the proper level, Alfred leaned out and grabbed the bags, at the same time releasing the control rope. However, the bags continued their journey upward. Melvin, watching their progress upward made a hasty retreat from the truck bed and watched the proceeding intently. The bags continued upward in spite of Alfred's jiggling of the control rope in an effort to release the belt. The chain rattling as it wrapped around the pulley signaled immanent doom. The ascending feedbags reached the pulley, the rope tore, and the four bags of grain fell back down on the truck bed. By the time the mess was cleaned up, the rope repaired, and the belt dressing removed, they could have unloaded two truckloads of grain, three bags at a time.

On July 4, 1941, heavy thunderstorms swept through the Weaverland Valley, drenching the soil, and halting the fieldwork. The next morning the neighborhood men and boys were visiting at Trupe's Mill. The men were visiting in the office and the boys were playing together in the mill. The boys were fooling around with the main upright power shaft that came up through the floor from the water turbine below and powered the whole mill. Lloyd Burkholder's wet coat somehow got wrapped on this shaft and Lloyd started to twirl around with this rapidly-spinning shaft. Right alongside the upright shaft was another shaft, which also came up the floor about three feet and had a wheel on top of it. This second shaft was the control for the water gate, which supplied the amount of water to the turbine below, controlling its speed. When Lloyd was entangled in the power shaft, his leg and arms were hitting the control shaft on every revolution. Fortunately, his head was above the height of the control shaft. Alfred Trupe was also among the playing boys, and he quickly tried to shut off the flow of water to the turbine to stop the shaft. In his excitement, Alfred first turned the wheel the wrong way, thus speeding up the shaft, before he got the turbine shut off. When the shaft came to a halt, Lloyd fell to the floor like a bundle of rags.

Boy's Legs And Arms Broken When Caught In Shaft

Lloyd Burkholder, fourteen, of East Earl R. D. 1, received fractures of both arms and both legs Friday when caught in the upright main shaft at the grist mill owned by Samuel Trupe, East Earl township. He was admitted to Lancaster General hospital where attendants said Friday night his condition was fair.

The youth and some other boys were playing at the mill, according to reports, Friday morning about 9:30 o'clock when Lloyd's coat caught in the shaft. He was twirled around and carried to the upper shaft when Alfred Trupe, son of the owner of the mill, quickly shut off the water wheel and rushed to the lad's aid.

Michael Burkholder, father of the injured youth, took him to the office of Dr. J. M. Wenger, of Terre Hill, where he received first aid and then took him to the hospital. The youth also received cuts on his right leg and body bruises.

Lancaster Intelligencer Journal, July 5, 1941.

Michael Burkholder, Lloyd's father, rushed Lloyd to Dr. Wenger in Terre Hill where he received first aid. Then he was hastened to the Lancaster General Hospital, were he was admitted. Lloyd had fractures on both arms and legs and had numerous cuts and bruises.

After a six-week stay in the hospital, he came home and over time fully recuperated. This accident interested the safety officials of the state. They made a visit to the mill and required that numerous changes be made. Shielding of moving parts, safety railings, and handrails at the steps were some of the required changes.[12]

During the hot summer months, the local boys would congregate and swim in the millrace after a hard day of work in the sun. There was an element of danger present. When the two water gates were open, they created a suction that pulled anything near it through the water gate. The force of the falling water had created a large pool on the downstream side of the water gate.

Usually the swimmers stayed well upstream of the water gates. However, when groups of young boys are together there is a tendency toward mischief. The water gates were open one beautiful summer evening when some neighborhood boys were sitting on the concrete walkway right above the water gate where the two control wheels were located and used to open and close the gate. The boys were sitting with their feet hanging in the rushing water, enjoying the strong tug it placed on their feet, watching the water exit the gate and arch into the churning pool below.

---

[12] On December 12, 1968, Lloyd Burkholder was ordained to the ministry at Fairview Mennonite Church in Lebanon County, Pennsylvania.

The discussion switched from the local happenings to daring each other. Alfred Trupe dived in the water right above the water gate. Holding his breath, he let the suction and force of the water carry him through the water gate and eject him in the pool below. There he swam to the shore, much to the awe of the rest of the boys. However, when word of his son's bravo reached his father, Samuel, it was replaced with a warm spot on the seat of his pants

Strong Men??

When work came to a halt because of rainy weather it seemed that all the neighborhood philosophers and their sons gathered at the mill. The water was high; in fact, it was at what we would call a flood stage. The water was almost up to the bottom of the concrete bridge which spanned the Conestoga River. Groups of men were watching the water rushing past. Bart Lehman and Joseph Hurst were daring each other to go for a swim in the boiling and churning floodwater. Some men tried to discourage Joe, telling him it was foolhardy. This went back and forth, and after a while, Joe Hurst jumped in the raging current. He was instantly swept downstream. Downstream from the bridge, the Conestoga made a sweeping left-hand turn. Joe managed to work himself over into the flooded pasture and out of the raging main steam of the current. He came back to the mill looking a bedraggled sight, but realized he was lucky to be alive.

Joseph Hurst was not only a strong swimmer. He was employed by the mill and enjoyed walking about the mill carrying a 100-pound bag of grain under each arm and grasping another 100-pound bag of grain by his teeth. If an audience were present, with a little encouragement, or an indication that he would not have the strength, Joe would climb up the steps carrying this heavy burden.

Apparently, the fame of a strong man working at Trupe's Mill reached the big city of Reading. One day a car pulled into the parking lot, and two beefy, well-muscled men came into the office asking for this brawny, strong mill worker. Joe Hurst was called and the two men from Reading sized him up, and challenged him to a fight.

Joe Hurst made the right move. He took the humble road, realizing that just as there are proper places to show physical strength, there are also proper places to show moral strength. The Reading boys considered this an act of weakness, and were quite vocal about it, but they returned to Reading unchallenged.

Joe was not above a lively tussle with his fellow mill workers. Bartey Lehman and Joe got into a friendly tussle in the mill office one winter evening. The activity got quite feisty, and in the ensuing commotion, the lighted stove was knocked over. The stovepipe came crashing down, filling the air with black soot.

The tussle was quickly forgotten as the participants and the spectators hustled to place things back into their proper places, before more damage occurred.

Electric Power Comes to the Valley

When the electric line came to the mill, Michael Burkholder also decided to take advantage of its convenience. Up to this point, the water in the house was pumped by hand from a well near the front porch. They got all the water to wash clothes or dishes from a cistern under the washhouse. They supplied the animals in the barn with water from another well in front of the barn. A pump powered by a hit and miss gasoline engine pumped water into a tank attached to the ceiling of the barn. From here, the water flowed by gravity to the livestock. The engine had to be started daily to fill the tank. This was usually the boys' chore, and had to be watched closely that it did not overrun and make a mess in the barn.

Michael hired Kelly Witmer to wire the house and barn for electricity. Apparently, Witmer had not perfected his understanding of how electricity worked. He ran wires, putting in lights and receptacles, twisted the wire ends together, and taped them. When the time came to turn the switches on the fuses just blew. Titus, as an interested young lad who later would become an electrician, gathered up the blown fuses and saved them. They were something new, a novelty in that day and age. When Kelly realized what Titus was doing, he became alarmed by the amount of blown fuses in Titus' collection. Then Kelly began throwing the blown fuses into the barnyard or garden instead of dropping them on the floor.

• 69 •

Finally, Kelly Witmer's son came and straightened everything out. The bill for wiring the whole farm was $126. This did not include the new electric refrigerator, electric iron, and electric wringer washer for Emma. The barn water was now pumped by electricity instead of the gasoline engine, but the water used in the house was still pumped by hand. If the monthly electric bill went over the power company's $3.00 minimum, there were instant repercussions and a lecture about leaving the lights on when they are not needed.

• *Chapter Eleven* •

Road Walkers

In the days before welfare, food stamps, poor people's homes, and a whole host of other programs to assist the needy, the Conestoga Valley was not only home to the industrious farmers. There were also the poor and homeless, often known as road walkers, because they walked the roads, stopping at farms, asking for food, tobacco, or anything else they needed. These poor people were accepted occupants of the valley and were taken for granted. They were an integral part of the community and no one questioned their existence, for as long as people could remember there were always these "bums" as they were called. In times past, there had been man and wife road walkers accepting the gifts of the farmers of the Weaverland Valley. The Mennonite housewives had a reputation of never refusing these unfortunate souls' request for food. The road walkers scrounged the countryside for their meager needs and had a few semi-official places reserved for them to congregate.

I recall as a lad, going to grandfather's house, and on the way home swinging into the Old Order Weaverland Church yard. Father used to shine the headlights of the car into the southwest stall of the buggy shed. Rain or shine, winter and summer, as many as six to ten bedraggled men, were patiently sitting around their open fire, with a brewing pot of coffee, and ignoring our intrusion. In the summer, we could also see them bedded down on the ground, scattered around the churchyard.

The Old Order Weaverland Mennonite Church had two horse shelters on the southwest corners, which were claimed by the road walkers. One could drive into the church yard almost anytime, day or night, and see these unfortunate men sitting around an open fire, brewing some coffee, and discussing who knows what. The walls of the first two stalls of the open-fronted building were decorated with all the meager belongings of its inhabitants. Broken pans, heavy winter coats, cloth bags or satchels, a shiny hubcap or two salvaged from a ditch, and anything else salvaged from the dumps scattered across the valley. The dilapidated shed across from Lichty's Church and in an old lime pit in Weaverland Road were two other congregating spots for these homeless, unfortunate souls.

When the weather would turn cold, they would ask a farmer to sleep in their barn. An unwritten rule, honored by all, was that the road walker would give his host his matches. The farmer's fear of a barn fire from a lit cigar was very real, and in this way, the road walker was conveying his respect for the farmer's concern. The road walker would make a nest in the warm hay, spend the night, and the next morning present himself for his matches. The housewife would almost invariably have a hearty breakfast prepared for their unshaven guest, to be eaten on the porch, before he headed out the farm lane. They were never asked into the house, as their hygiene was not questionable. Their odor proved it was nonexistent. If a hostess had company invited for Sunday dinner, she could expect a couple of road walkers to appear shortly after the meal was finished, having been notified by the numerous buggies sitting outside the barnyard. These uninvited but welcome visitors were graciously served a plateful of leftovers of the ample dinner.

On one of these occasions, a visiting mother had wrapped a child's severely soiled diaper in an old newspaper, and placed it on the porch to pick up on the way home. Throughout the afternoon, numerous road walkers visited, enjoying the leftover Sunday dinner on the porch. When the company started to go home, the mother came for the soiled diaper, but it was nowhere to be found, and she had to leave for home without it.

The next morning the newspaper and the soiled diaper were found at the end of the lane. Apparently, a road walker had thought the neatly wrapped package was for him; but instead he was in for an odorous revelation when he opened his surprise package. It was a common practice to wrap some food in a newspaper for them to eat later in the day.

The road walkers not only enjoyed the food, but also read the newspaper as they wasted their days away.

One road walker, who frequented the area of Trupe's Mill, was known as Pegleg. His pegleg tipped with steel, drove the neighborhood dogs into frenzy. The dogs always foretold his coming long before he was seen, and would torment him. His pegleg was nicked and scratched where the dogs had bitten and gnawed at it. For some reason, the dogs hated the sound that his false leg made as he traveled along the roads of the Conestoga Valley.

The Weaverland Valley had the distinction of having a road walking team. The Thomsons, a man and wife road walking team, frequented the Valley's roads looking for handouts. The story is told that Emma purchased a pound can of coffee that was not good. She tried to brew some numerous times, but it was terrible. In one instance, she gave a road walker a meal and some of this bitter coffee. After he had enjoyed his meal on the porch, he knocked on the door. As he returned the plate and utensils, he thanked Emma for the delicious meal. However, he also added, "The coffee was terrible."

This offending can of coffee sat in Emma's cupboard until she got tired of seeing it. A day or so later, other road walkers arrived. He not only received a generous meal, but they also took an almost full tin of coffee along to enjoy around their evening campfire.

Most of the time these men were left to their own devices, but occasionally their presence gave the young boys opportunity to torment them. On one occasion, a few boys were throwing mud balls at the road walkers off the bank of the old Lime pit on Weaverland Road. At first, the road walkers ignored the boys, and the boys continued their harassment. Finally, one of the road walkers stood up, pulled a ten-inch knife, and started up the bank. The boys suddenly remember they had other things to do.

Victory, But Not Victorious

Not all the road walkers were satisfied with food or shelter. One road walker had developed a liking to alcohol. This particular road walker also requested money—not well accepted among the farmers.

This specific road walker was making his request known to the homemaker at a prosperous farm. The homemaker declined the request for money, but offered to prepare a sandwich for him to eat which he grudgingly accepted. The road walker placed the sandwich in his pocket and ambled out the farm lane, and up the street. When he was out of sight of the house, he took the sandwich out of his pocket, peeled back the newspaper and checked what type of sandwich the homemaker had prepared for him. Apparently, he was not satisfied with its contents, because with a careless shrug, he threw the uneaten sandwich into the ditch alongside the road and continued on his way unperturbed.

This whole scene was keenly observed. The farmer was in the field hauling manure, but had been keeping close tabs on the happenings at his house. He had witnessed the road walker's arrival, and by this man's reputation had surmised what was happening. Seeing the unappreciated gift of food tossed in the gutter was not in accordance with his reputation of frugality. Being a man of action, he urged his horses to a trot and swung out on the road. He speared the sandwich in the gutter with his manure fork, which had just previously been used to load his spreader and pursued the road walker. As the fast-moving team approached the pursued, yet ignorant and unsuspecting road walker, he turned and was surprised when the team came to a sudden stop. The driver of the team stood up, forcefully jabbed the manure fork with the discarded sandwich still speared on it, right in front of the road walker's face. "Eat it," came the stern command. The road walker hesitated, but the manure fork jabbed and poked directly in front of his face. Slowly, he reached up, took the sandwich off the manure fork, and slowly ate it, his eyes never leaving the glowering farmer's face. When the last crumb was eaten, the farmer, with a victorious smirk commanded his horses, "Giddap." As the horses turned around, the victorious smirk was quickly removed. A sobering frown took its place as he considered the road walker's parting question, " Would you like to see your barn burn down some dark night?"

Welsh Mountain Wayfarers

Occasionally another element of society would also venture into the Weaverland Valley. About five miles south in the crannies and hollows of the Welsh Mountains lived a group of colored folks. They were descendants of escaped Civil War slaves, who had settled in the seclusion of the mountains in the mid 1800s. The people in the valley viewed these people with distrust, presuming they lived in supposed vice and poverty. While the road walkers were considered honest, it was not so with the Welsh Mountain people. Periodically, a family with their children and a skinny horse and wagon would come down into the valley. They also came to beg and at times sell huckleberries which were numerous in the Welsh Mountains.

One summer a Welsh Mountain family stopped their skinny horse on the road, and the mother with a child started to walk in the lane. The men were usually along, but invariably the woman and child came to the door to request their needs. Trixie, a large German Shepherd police dog, barred her way and chased her back to the wagon. The Burkholder boys, attracted by the dog's hubbub came and hid behind the lilac bush just as she climbed back into the wagon. The boys heard the Negro father asking his wife, "What's wrong? It's only a dog." The disgruntled woman then said, "Then you go."

The Welsh Mountain Negro hopped out of his dilapidated spring wagon and started in the farm lane. About halfway into the lane stood Trixie, growling with his hair standing up on his back, and a little further back was the lilac bush with Melvin and Raymond hiding behind it. About 25 feet from Trixie, the Negro stopped and tried to sweet talk him, but every time he took one step forward, so did the dog as it was hissed on by the boys. Finally, the Negro gave up and turned back to the spring wagon. As soon as he turned, Trixie charged and chased him the whole way back to his wagon. He scrambled on and went elsewhere for the provisions they desired.

Steaming Tobacco Beds

Tobacco was a labor-intensive crop. Early in the spring, the tobacco was seeded in carefully prepared beds near the farmstead. Before the seeds were planted, however, the bed was "steamed" to kill any weed seeds, which would have choked out the tender tobacco seedlings. Several farmers had old steam boilers, some mounted on trucks, or an old traction steam engine, which went around the neighborhood steaming tobacco beds.

Large pans about eight feet square were placed over the future tobacco beds and pressed into the soil. Steam was made in the boiler, but instead of utilizing the steam for power, it was was piped out to the pans. The steam penetrated the soil, sterilizing it, and making it mellow. It took about twenty minutes a pan until they had to be moved. This job usually went on day and night. The engineer needed the farmer's help to move the pans and used the steam whistle to summon him for assistance.

• *Chapter Twelve* •

Phares Martin's 1926 Mack Truck

In 1941, Phares Martin purchased H.M. Stauffer's 1926 Mack truck. He used a thrashing rig, powered by an old steam traction engine, to steam tobacco beds. Top speed on a steam traction engine was 2.5 miles an hour and he wished to go faster from one customer to another. Phares removed the wheels and engine apparatus from his old steam traction engine, and placed the boiler on the 1926 Mack truck. With this increased mobility, he could take care of more customers. He steamed tobacco beds all over the Weaverland Valley, then moved up to the west side of Ephrata where he had recently purchased a farm for his son Weaver Martin.

Eventually Weaver and his brother Clarence "Toddy" purchased this rig. They continued steaming tobacco beds, taking over the business their father had started.

On October 24, 1948, the steamers came to Michael Burkholder to prepare his tobacco beds for the next spring. However, there was a problem. The Mack truck's axle was broken, and it could not go under its own power. Michael hooked his Oliver 70 to the truck and pulled it to the location where he planned to place his tobacco beds. The next day when they were finished steaming, they towed the Mack to Frank Martins so that he could continue his work.

In 1962, Weaver Martin's son, Clarence, purchased the business and continued steaming tobacco beds until 1977. The rig sat in a shed

• 77 •

Phares Martin's 1926 Mack Truck—before and after.

until 1984 when the boiler was sold at Weaver Martin's farm sale. The Mack truck was kept in the family, and in later years beautifully restored.

Today the truck is used to take people for rides. When father, in his youth, was helping Toddy steam the tobacco beds at his home, never in his wildest imaginations would he have thought he would ride this same truck when he was 76 years old.

One day when dad was reminiscing about days gone by, he remembered Toddy and his steamer on a Mack truck. Realizing where the truck was, arrangements were made to take him and the rest of the family on an outing. The same truck which was part of a maturing teenager's life, was also used later in life for an outing.

◆ Chapter Thirteen ◆

Neighborhood Challenges

In any close-knit community there is an element of rivalry. Who is the first to plant corn? Whose hay was rained on in the thunderstorm last night? These things and much more were discussed when the neighborhood philosphers gathered at Trupe's Mill. Everyone enjoyed when one of the neighbors "got one" on one of the other neighbors. These were all in good-natured fun which livened up the long hours and hard work.

Joseph Hurst was husking corn with his team and a flatbed wagon with low sides. When traveling to the shocked cornfield, Joseph had to pass right in front of Reuben Hurst's tobacco stripping room window. With a grin on his face, he urged his team to a full gallop. Just before they shot across the front of Reuben's stripping room window, Joseph lay down on the wagon bed, completely out of sight. Reuben seeing the seemingly driverless team gallop past with the clattering wagon behind, dropped his tobacco stalk, and rushed out of the stripping room. Forgetting coat and hat, he jumped into his pickup and raced after Joseph's team. However, as he pulled aside the speeding team, Joseph stood up with a large smirk and waved. Reuben probably heard about this for a while, or at least until another incident took place to regale about.

In those days, corn was cut off by hand and then shocked in large upright bundles. There was always some friendly rivalry to see which neighbor could finish first.

• 80 •

One year the neighbors were all busy shocking corn, and it appeared that Michael was in no hurry to get started. When Michael was asked about it, he just brushed them off.

However, Michael had a plan up his sleeve. Instead of starting to shock corn around the outside edge of his cornfield where all could see his progress, he started in the middle of the field. The middle of the field was all shocked and unnoticed by his neighbors. Then one morning, Michael shocked the outside cornrows, and was done. He was the first farmer in the Valley to have his corn all harvested.

Harry Martin had a silo-filling rig and went around the neighborhood custom-filling silos. Harry had a lot of confidence in his equipment. He bragged that no one could stall his new Oliver and his belt-driven Denlinger ensilage cutter with a sixteen-inch throat into the cutter head. Well, all boasts have to be proven, especially by the adventurous. At Martin Eberly's, a plan was hatched. Joseph and Reuben Hurst loaded their wagon very carefully and precisely, with the goal of easing the unloading. There was a crew of men in the cornfield hand-cutting the corn and laying it on the ground. From there, it was pitched on a flatbed wagon and hauled to the silo. There it was hand-fed into the ensilage cutter which chopped the corn and blew it into the silo.

Joseph and Reuben planned to put an all-out effort to stall Harry's new Oliver tractor. They wanted a load of corn that would unload easily. They layered their load so there would be no tugging and pulling stalks from under others. When loaded they drove to the silo nice and easy so the load of corn would stay nice and fluffy. They pulled up to the ensilage cutter and parked it just right for ease of unloading.

Harry, who tended his rig at the silo, engaged the clutch and the belt started spinning with a gentle whisper, as the ensilage cutter was brought up to speed.

Joseph and Reuben started pitching the corn on the ensilage cutter's table nice and easy. When they had developed a nice rhythm, working together smoothly, they stepped up the pace. The corn stalks flowed like clockwork from the wagon to the ensilage cutter, and the Oliver started to labor. Harry, who was puttering around the tractor, looked up questioningly, but confident that his equipment was not concerned. Meanwhile, Joseph and Reuben stepped up the pace again. At this pace, the corn had to be fed evenly, as their goal was not to clog up the ensilage cutter, but stall

· 81 ·

the tractor. They seemed to be succeeding. As the Oliver labored under the heavy load, the engine began to lose RPM. Harry came running to release the clutch, which powered the table feeding corn to the cutter head. However, one of the Hurst boys pushed Harry's hand away as he placed the last large handful of corn on the feeder table which brought the Oliver's engine to a stall. The long endless belt, one instant under full load, freed from the tension, whip-lashed from the pulleys, and slithered over the ground. Silence settled on the job site as some cut corn silage drifted down from the top of the silo, and a wisp of steam escaped from the stalled tractor's engine.

Harry and the Hurst brothers looked over the results of boasting and then the challenge to it. The belt had to be placed back on the equipment; the blower pipe was clogged; and the cutter head and feed rolls were chocked full of corn. All this had to be cleaned out by hand. An hour of hard dirty work—all extra work—lay ahead of them just because of a boast and the desire to prove a point!

Weaver Breaks His Wrist

One extremely cold January winter morning with the temperature, "ten below zero," Titus wanted to start the Farmall A tractor to do some farm chores. He tried to start the engine, but with the extreme cold the starter would not crank the engine fast enough to get it running. With teen-age enthusiasm, eighteen-year-old Weaver tried to help it along with the hand crank. With Titus pressing the starter, and Weaver cranking the engine with all his might, the engine sputtered to life. However, not before it backfired, spinning the crank backwards and breaking Weaver's wrist. For six weeks, he had an obvious reminder of the effect of that one bitter cold morning with a cast on his wrist and hand.

Overload

About 1942, Michael Burkholder made the decision to go into the dairy business.

Up to this point, they always had a family cow or two, and the milk not used for the family was separated. The cream was made into butter and the whey fed to the pigs. The barn had room for about eight cows, but no milkhouse was located on the farm. Hershey Milk Company was contacted and they said they would work with Michael until a milk-house was built. Michael purchased a new four-can Wilson milk cooler and put it into the wagon shed. He also purchased a few cows and they were in the milk business.

One day Michael, Raymond, and Lloyd, staked off the area where the new milkhouse was to be built. The boys were then given orders to dig a ditch for the foundation of the new building. Raymond and Lloyd pulled the spring wagon from the wagon shed and industriously began to dig the trench placing the dirt in the spring wagon. When the spring wagon was nicely loaded, one of the boys went to harness Bert and hook her in the spring wagon. The other lad continued digging, heaping the load higher and higher on the spring wagon.

When Bert was hooked up, both boys climbed up and sat in the spring wagon seat to take the dirt out and scatter it in the field. "Giddap Bert," came the command, and the heavy load started forward with the wooden wheels screeching in protest. So far, all was going fine! As they coaxed Bert into a trot around the bend in the lane, there was a sudden crack. The wagon came to an abrupt stop as the rear wheel collapsed completely and the heavily-loaded wagon sank to the axle. The stress and twist on the wagon caused the front wheel to also buckle under the weight of the heavy load.

Michael was called and he came and beheld the woeful scene. He viewed the smashed wheels, and observed the overloaded wagon bed. Turning to the boys, he stated his opinion which showed he understood how boys' minds operate. "Way too much weight, yet both of you got up in the spring wagon seat and wanted to ride!"

The boys had hopes that this was the end of the spring wagon. Nevertheless, Michael repaired the wheels and the spring wagon gave many more years of service.

Precious Memories

As Michael and Emma's children grew up, they were guided on the path of Christian living. When some of the older boys tried to take some parental authority on themselves and boss the younger brothers and sister, Michael usually would quote: ***When I was a child, I spake as a child, I understood as a child, I thought as a child: but when I became a man, I put away childish things***. 1 Corinthian 13:11

Michael also strongly discouraged his children to go the Pennsylvania Farm Show. He quoted Matthew 24:28 to raise conviction against the Farm Show: ***For wheresoever the carcase is, there will the eagles be gathered together***. Even after his boys were married and had their own farms, he pleaded with them not to attend the Farm Show.

World War II and the Weaverland Valley

Although the world was at war, life in the Weaverland Valley went on at its own unhurried pace. However, the fingers of unrest coiled into the valley in time. Gasoline was rationed, thus there was the temptation to use " Tractor Gas" intended for farm use in the automobiles. Sugar, shoes, and many other articles were rationed, and some things were simply not to be found. Nevertheless, the greatest fear by far was the draft, newly reinstated, requiring all eighteen year-olds and older men to register.

Melvin and Raymond both recall vivid memories of their individual trolley trips from Blue Ball to the Lancaster train station. From there they had their first train rides to Philadelphia for the required physical. Most of the boys on the train had no religious conviction, and were very rowdy. Raymond recalled how the boys were rocking the train coach in an attempt to derail the car. For the Mennonite boys, the situation was quite different. Not only did they have nonresistant convictions, they certainly did not want to attract attention and possibly get into trouble. After a day under the vigorous and strict regiment of military authority, all the boys went home subdued and thoughtful. For most of the boys, it was a foretaste of the military life before them. For a small group there was a vastly different thought. The day's events gave way to a hearty thankfulness for a hope of staying at home and working on the farm.

Lloyd was also part of a trainload of youth who went to Harrisburg for a military physical. Passing this physical made him available to serve his country. Fortunately, the United Sates Government recognized growing food for its citizens and its soldiers was a vital and very necessary service to the country. The boys requesting a farm deferment had to prove to the local draft board that service to the agricultural community was sufficient to merit a deferment. Michael and Lloyd requested a hearing with the local draft board and on the appointed day they appeared before the three-man committee.

They were armed with a paper signed by Doctor Wenger affirming Michael's problem with low blood pressure. Michael testified Lloyd was needed to help on the farm to make it successful. After some questions, Lloyd received his farm deferment.

Life for the youth was subdued during World War II. Pleasure driving was strictly curtailed and many youth stayed home. When attending a youth gathering, all the youth of a certain area car-pooled. It was common for boys to hear some derogatory remarks when driving through town about their draft status. Air raid drills in the surrounding towns sent the wailing sirens echoing throughout the Weaverland Valley. The wailing siren signaled the people in the towns to a blackout drill. All lights were to be turned off. The streetlights were turned off. If driving, you were required to stop and turn off the headlights and wait. The authorities were preparing the people for attack from enemy airplanes!

Over this time, Melvin was working for John F. Martin, helping to tend a stand in Philadelphia on Wednesdays and Saturdays. Certain food items were very scarce in towns. A line extending a block long would form an hour before the stands opened at 7:00 a.m. Food like butter would soon be sold out, and some was usually hid for special customers and friends who could not show up early.

One evening, about dark, John F. Martin sent Melvin to a farmer to catch some chickens to butcher the next day with plans to take the dressed chickens to market. When Melvin arrived, he found the farmer guarding his chickens with a revolver, giving him a scare. After Melvin told the farmer his mission and paid him with cash, they caught the fat broilers for the next day's butchering.

To purchase some things you had to have ration stamps. Each family was allowed a certain amount of stamps which then gave you the right to purchase those products. Sugar was rationed causing some farmers to grow sugar cane. There also was the temptation of buying "black market" sugar, which was smuggled around the authorities and illegal.

• 85 •

◆ Chapter Fourteen ◆

School Problems in the Weaverland Valley

The years of 1937 to 1954 were trying times for the Old Order Mennonite families who had older school children. The state was enforcing compulsory school laws which went beyond what the Mennonites thought was needed for an education. In those years, there was a constant uncertainly of where they stood when they kept their children home after they finished eighth grade.

The first bill requiring compulsory attendance in Pennsylvania schools was presented to the Legislature in 1874, but failed to pass. In 1893, a similar bill was passed by the Legislature, but was vetoed by Governor Pattison, who felt it an invasion of personal liberty, and would incite much civil strife, controversy, and opposition. The advocates of compulsory education in Pennsylvania was persistent and in 1895 secured the passage of a compulsory education bill. Children between the ages of eight to thirteen were required to attend school at least sixteen weeks of the six-month term.

In 1899, the term extended to seven months, and in 1901, the age limit was extended to sixteen years with an exemption for those older than thirteen who were engaged in lawful employment. In these years, the laws were on the books, but were loosely enforced and often ignored by many townships.

On May 29, 1907, the compulsory laws were strengthened to state that all children between the ages of eight and sixteen were required to

Schoolman At E. Earl Twp. Quits Over Jailings

Michael W. Burkholder, East Earl R1, a member of the East Earl Twp. School Board for 16 years, resigned last night during a regular board meeting in the Blue Ball school.

Burkholder, who served as the board's vice president, submitted his resignation in writing stating he resigned "because his conscience will not permit him to send these people to jail."

The resignation of Burkholder,

Turn To Page 6 For More Of DIRECTOR

Lancaster Intelligencer Journal clippings.

DIRECTOR

(Continued From Page One)

a member of the Weaverland Mennonite Church came as one East Earl Twp father John J Martin Jr., New Holland R2 was released from prison yesterday where he was sentenced for failure to send his 14-year-old son to school.

ASKS WORK PERMIT

Also last night, a township resident Wallis Stauffer, New Holland RD requested a work permit for his 14-year-old son Stauffer after being told that the permit must be secured from the county superintendent of schools, said if he cannot get a permit he won't send his son to school anyway.

Burkholder's resignation on the East Earl Twp. board was the first due to the Amish situation although one former member and president, Elam H. Zimmerman, Blue Ball, resigned some time ago when the State Department of Public Instruction ordered the inclusion of Honey Brook borough and Honey Brook Twp. into the Eastern jointure of which East Earl Twp. is a part.

A special session was called for tonight to finish routine business which the board was unable to do last night.

---

attend school continuously. Children were required to be present during the entire term in their respective district while school was in session. Children between the ages of fourteen to sixteen who could read and write English intelligently, and were gainfully engaged in a useful occupation were exempted from the school system. In 1919, 1925, and 1931, the school attendance laws were strengthened, but in ways which did not greatly affect the Old Order Mennonites.

In 1937, the compulsory attendance age was raised to eighteen years of age in city districts and fifteen years in rural districts, and the term was lengthened to nine months.

The Amish and Mennonite communities held various meetings and agreed they could not abide with this infringement from the world on their children. Many, but not all, withheld their fourteen-year-old children from school, or filled out questionable forms of domestic or farm permit exemptions. The school authorities signed these permits, wanting to keep peace, and an uneasy truce existed until the fall of 1950.

When the school term started in September 1950, most local school authorities refused to sign the domestic or farm exceptions because of direction from the state. This placed the school boards and the Amish and Mennonite families in a quandary. The consensus among the Amish and Mennonites was to keep their fourteen-year-olds who had completed eighth grade home from school. Most fathers who kept their fourteen-year-olds home, were fined. Since they felt payment of the fine was confessing to guilt, they refused to do so and instead went to jail. However, a mysterious unknown person paid their fines which kept them out of prison.

A total of 39 Amish and Mennonite parents were prosecuted with some jailed for their faith. After these prosecutions and with the pleading of local school directors, some parents sent their fourteen-year-olds back to school, but many remained at home. The school authorities hesitated to prosecute the parents again, thus the uneasy truce continued through the rest of that school term.

Since the school boards were divided into districts, those with a higher concentration of Amish were affected the most. Some township officials simply removed the names of Amish and Mennonite scholars who had graduated from eighth grade from the school attendance charts, thus effectively taking them out of the school system.

This condition of disquiet between the State School Board versus patrons continued for the terms of 1951-52 and 1952-53. A few prosecutions in the beginning of the year and then a "wait-and-see" attitude for the rest of the term occurred, with many fourteen-year-old scholars staying at home.

On July 21, 1953, Dr. Francis B. Haas, state Superintendent of Public Instruction gave the seven townships plagued with the Old Order and Amish fourteen-year-old school attendance problems an ultimatum. Either enforce the compulsory school attendance laws or else forfeit state subsidies. Nearly $120,000 of state school funding was consequently withheld from seven townships when school began in September. East Earl Township was expecting $20,208 to help fund the 1953-54 school term, which was not forthcoming until they could prove they were enforcing the school attendance laws. This placed the school board directors in a precarious situation, forcing them to prosecute those who failed to send their fourteen- to fifteen-year-old children to school. A rash of prosecutions followed with many fathers spending a five-day term in jail. In many cases, local businesses or concerned neighbors paid the fine, thus sparing the father from his jail term.

Dwight Eisenhower was campaigning for president during the summer of 1953. One of his campaign stops was at the New Holland Sales Stables. Many Mennonites and Amish who resided in the Conestoga Valley attended this event. During his speech, Dwight Eisenhower made a comment, which attracted many plain people and swayed their votes. He boldly stated, "If I am elected president, the sending of the Amish to jail will stop!"

These turbulent school years were a difficult time for Michael Burkholder. It was standard practice for each school district to have a conservative Mennonite on the school board. Michael Burkholder served in this position for sixteen years. In the November 1949 election, Michael had only nine more votes than his rival did. He and Clarence Renninger were reelected to the school board. This work required many evenings and days of work. Records show that some weeks there were three meetings a week concerning school matters. There were also director's meetings to attend at Millersville College in Millersville and numerous trips to Harrisburg. In the middle of the summer, a meeting was held "to set the taxes" and before school started, the directors had to deliver the supplies to the individual schools.

Leon Attends a School Meeting

All of these meetings apparently aroused the curiosity of Michael's son, Leon. One time when Michael was preparing to attend another school meeting, Leon snuck out to his father's car and lay on the floor behind the front seat. Michael came out, drove to Blue Ball School where the meeting was held, and parked the car.

Meanwhile at home one of the boys asked, "Where is Leon?" A hasty search revealed he was not there. The whole family quickly mobilized for a thorough search of the farmstead. However, Leon was nowhere to be found.

Emma did not know what to do. She hoped that Leon had gone with Michael, yet she could not be certain. They had no telephone, and no other vehicle. Should she go to the neighbors and ask them to go to Blue Ball School and see if Leon was there?

Paul and Etta Good (left) and Ada Mae and Raymond Burkholder at Ammon and Frances Weaver's wedding.

Emma decided to wait until Michael came home. She and the rest of the family waited apprehensively. Finally, Michael turned into the driveway. Emma and the whole family watched him drive by the house, and into the wagon shed where he parked his car. There was no little boy sitting alongside of Michael, and all feared the worst. Leon was still missing.

Michael got out of the car and started walking to the house while the rest of the family came to meet him. However, suddenly the back door of Michael's car door opened. Everyone's attention turned to the car, and out came Leon. Relief swept through Emma and Leon's brothers and sisters. Michael, who had no clue on what was going on was perplexed, but was soon told the story. Leon had spent the whole evening lying in the car, most of the time lying on the floor. His worst moment was when another board member parked his car right next to Michael's car. When that board member got out of his car, Leon feared discovery.

Michael was serving as Vice-President of the East Earl School Board during 1953. On September 24, 1553, Emma's diary shows that

Michael had a visitor. John J. Martin, of the "Thirty Fiver" Church, who was just released from a jail sentence for keeping his fourteen-year-old son home on the farm. John, along with ten other Amish and Mennonites were in a quandary on the school issue. It would be interesting to know their conversation.

Four days later, on September 28, 1953, Michael resigned from his position on the school board. Apparently, this visit was the incident which convinced Michael that he could no longer serve on the school board. He handed in a written resignation stating that his conscience does not permit him to send his fellow brethren to jail. His resignation was recorded in the *Lancaster Intelligencer Journal*.

• *Chapter Fifteen* •

Church Involvements

The Mennonite Aid Ordinance

The Mennonite fire aid plan that the Old Order Mennonites use today fulfills the scripture verse in Galatians 6:2: **Bear ye one another's burdens and so fulfill the law of Christ**. This plan has evolved over the years. When a brother had a loss in the early Mennonite church, it was announced in the church. The deacons would choose certain men as collectors and they would visit each member of the church. The member would contribute whatever he felt was his share.

This plan worked fine until the depression years of the 1930s. Farms were growing larger and more machinery was used. When a loss occurred and the collections made, the deacons would occasionally discover there was not enough of money collected to cover the loss.

On September 17, 1941, John W. Martin near Martindale had a fire where his barn, implement shed, and chicken house, burned to the ground. The loss was estimated at $18,000. There was a collection held and it was insufficient. The collectors were sent out a second time to glean more funds for John Martin's loss.

Michael Burkholder was one of the collectors sent out on this collection. He came home rather discouraged, and related how he visited a supposedly wealthy farmer. At first he did not want to give anything, but after Michael questioned him on how he expected his church brother, John Martin, to be reimbursed for his loss if all the brethren took that course, the brother then did contribute some small change he was carrying in his pocket.

There were those who suspected that the wage earners were shouldering more than there fair share of the burden. This was during the years of the depression and money was tight for the farmers and business owners. But if a person had a job, he received a paycheck and possibly has some money around when the collectors came. The farmers and business owners had equity, but no cash when the collectors arrived.

At the Old Order Mennonites' fall conference, the deacons decided to instruct the collectors to keep close records of who gave how much. This was done and it was discovered that what some had suspected was true. The property owners were not giving enough in relation to their holdings. There was a definite need for improvement and organization.

Moses Kurtz took the initiative and visited an Amish man who was involved with their plan to see how they conducted their fire plan. He took some ideas from them, and came up with a plan to present to his brethren. A meeting was held and Samuel H. Good was elected as chairperson. The plan initiated at that meeting is still in effect today.

The new Mennonite Aid Ordinance was submitted at the spring conference and approved. Anyone who desired not to participate in the new plan was still eligible to ask for help using the old plan, and a free-will offering would be held, but everyone was encouraged to use the new modified system. A deacon's helper, called a book holder, was appointed for each church. They were to assist the deacon in the bookwork that this new plan required.

In the new plan, each property owner was instructed to visit a book holder and record a value for the property to be insured. Each person set his own property values. When a person had a loss, this value was used to set the loss. The loss is compared with the total asset recorded in the whole church brotherhood and a percentage or millage is agreed upon. Then the deacon appoints collectors to visit the laity and collect the funds

In the first year, six million dollars worth of property were placed into this plan. Using this as an example, we can see that a 1% millage on six million would have generated $60,000. A person who had their home assessed at $10,000 would have been expected to contribute $100, while the farmer's share with $100,000, would have been $1,000. If anyone felt obligated to give more, they were free to do so.

Michael was designated as a book holder, and was involved in this program from its beginning in 1942, until his son John took the responsibilities in the early 1970s. But it is recalled that initially he possibly took this responsibility unwillingly. When he was appointed by the deacons he had excuses why he should not serve. But an ordained man present pointed that maybe sometime he would come into a position where he could make no excuses, pointing to ordinations. Michael then let the matter rest, and accepted.

Ordinations

Michael was in the lot twice for minister and once for deacon. On April 26, 1928, 27-year-old Michael was one of eight candidates when John B. Weaver was ordained minister.

Both the Old Order Weaverland Conference and the Brick Weaverland Mennonite Churches had ordinations planned for December 1940. Michael and Emma were members of the Old Order group, and Michael's brother, John, who lived on the homestead across the Conestoga River were members at the Weaverland Brick Church. This caused their Mother, Susan to remark, "The lot might hit on both sides of the Conestoga."

Michael's younger brother, John, was ordained as a minister in the Weaverland Mennonite Brick Church on December 4, 1940.

Being selected as a candidate for the lot weighed heavy on Michael's mind before the ordination. He often sang the song, "My Jesus as Thou Wilt," *Church and Sunday School Hymnal,* #475.

On December 22, 1940, there were nine candidates including Michael, when Joseph O. Weaver was ordained minister.

When Henry Z. Martin was ordained deacon for Weaverland and Martindale on June 7, 1951, Michael was also one of the nine candidates. Henry Z. Martin recalls that Bishop Joseph O. Weaver set the books on the singing table to determine the lot. Apparently, he was not satisfied, and he came back and switched the books situated in front of Michael and Henry. Each candidate took the book in front of him, and the lot fell on Henry!

When Michael, Emma, and his family were on the way to the ordination the boys in the back seat were discussing Frank Hurst's new Chrysler car. Apparently they were not as concerned as they should have been about the forthcoming proceedings at Church, until Michael rebuked them, saying, "We will not talk about cars on the way to church."

An interesting side note was that Michael's son, Titus, and Anna

Sensenig had married the preceding Saturday of the ordination. They were on a wedding trip to Niagara Falls when the ordination took place. When they were looking for a motel for the night in Bradford County, they hit a deer, damaging their car rather seriously. A local resident in the vicinity of the accident took pity on them, and invited them to stay for the night. The kind-hearted family offered them a sofa bed to spend the night. When they woke up the next morning, they found the family's housecat also enjoyed visitors, as it had snuggled in with them during the night.

Michael Accepts Song Leading Position

About 1950, Michael was asked if he would consider leading songs at church services. He accepted, which meant he would now sit at the singers table in front of the church. The boys at home got weary of his practicing songs at home around the farm. German songs were still used frequently, so he had to become familiar with songs in both languages. Michael's favorite hymn was "By Cool Siloam's Shady Rill" *Mennonite Hymns*, Number 402.

The services at Weaverland Mennonite Church traditionally closed with both a song in German and a song in English. As more and more people became unfamiliar with the German language, the issue to discontinue the German song arose. Whenever changing to all English singing was discussed, Michael defended keeping it as it was. However, on one of Michael and Anna's weekend trips to Canada, German singing at Weaverland Church was discontinued. The next Sunday after they returned, Weaverland had all English singing. When Michael mentioned about the change, one of the other song leaders quipped, "If you want to continue singing German songs, you will have to stay here." The subject was dropped.

As a young man, Melvin joined a singing quartet. Earl Martin, Ivan Fox, Ivan Lutz, and Melvin enjoyed visiting bedridden people, weddings, and Brethren Churches, singing in their quartet.

Ivan Lutz, another member of the quartet, was a small man with a resounding bass voice. When the quartet was practicing one evening at Melvin's home, Michael was upstairs. He purposely came downstairs to see this man with a deep bass voice. He was surprised to see a small slender man. The quartet recorded some songs on a wire recorder, which was later recorded again on a tape cassette. This cassette is still in Melvin's procession today.

• 95 •

◆ *Chapter Sixteen* ◆

Life's Experiences

Material for the Ladies

The young girls of the house always eagerly awaited the delivery of chicken feed. The feed truck was barely out the driveway before they were in the feed room looking at the bags containing the chicken feed. In those days of thrift and waste-not, the feedbags were recycled into dresses, pillowcases, curtains, and many other things.

The bags that the feed companies used had many different prints and designs on them. Many of the bags had large flowers or other objectionable designs which made them unsuitable for dress material. Occasionally they could collect the needed four bags of a suitable print, which would mean a new dress for one of the girls. The bags were shook out very good, turned inside out, and all the seams taken out. The material was washed and then it was ready to be sewn. Arlene learned her sewing skills, and made her first dress out of feedbag material.

Oliver Days

Michael was a diligent and efficient farmer. In 1948, he purchased a new Oliver 60 tractor from Farmersville Equipment located in Farmersville. Sometime later, Farmersville Equipment hosted an "Oliver Day" for all their customers. Michael was not sure about attending these affairs since they showed films which he considered frivolous. However, Edna, pleaded to attend and Michael finally relented.

When Michael, Edna, and Arlene arrived at "Oliver Day," the first thing they saw was a display of the door prizes to be awarded. Michael was going to pass by, but Edna, all eyes and ears in this new experience, wondered why he was refusing this opportunity. Ivan Nolt, the owner of the establishment, was standing nearby and watching the arrivals. He observed the conversation and interrupted with a calm, "Why sure you will sign up, Michael. You might even win something!" as he ushered Michael to the table. So reluctantly, Michael signed up for a door prize.

Wonder of all wonders, the next morning a telephone call came stating that Michael had won the Grand Prize. A brand new General Electric sweeper was his. All he had to do was pick it up. Edna was delighted. Not only had she convinced Michael to attend "Oliver Days." Now she could clean house with their "free" sweeper.

Frank and Harry Walker

Michael, Frank, and Leon, were repairing the barn floor. They had removed all the planks on the floor and were replacing them with new flooring. Earlier they had jacked up the main beam to level it for a nice level floor. In this portion of the project, the jack had slipped and injured Michael's hand.

Harry Walker, a fast-talking salesperson, and Michael were talking outside the barn while the boys were working inside. Frank, as a thirteen-year-old youth, was gingerly balancing himself as he stepped along one of the exposed floor beams while doing a creditable imitation of Harry Walker's fast-moving sales pitch. When he was in the middle of the beam, his performance suddenly went silent, when the beam cracked, broke, and dumped him in the cellar below.

Leon ran around the barn and into the cellar from an outside entrance. When he reached a crumbled and silent Frank, he did not know what to do. There were no obvious injuries, but Frank did not respond. Leon looked up through the uncovered beams to the open barn doors. Michael and Harry Walker were standing there, summoned by the noise. Michael finally said, "Just let him be. He is probably just knocked out." Sure enough, in a moment or two Frank groggily got to his feet, having no injuries.

JANUARY 16

1955 "Sun fair we were at home the boys were at church Pop doesn't feel so good Weather were here
19 This afternoon Melvina Joyce was here a while Melvina stayed a while Too tonight John was here
19 a little Pop had a heart attack at 6.30 and 9 o'clock they took him to the hospital in the ambulance

1956 Mon partly cloudy we washed Edna worked a little we visited Nelson Martin at the hospital
19 Pharis & Edna were in with him then we visited Ray Newswenger Too He is out of bed now

JANUARY 17

1955 "Mon it was at the hospital until after time Pop is very sick he is in an Oxygen tent and they
19 feel him through the veins

1955 Tue it snowed last night but is clear now & windy they scraped the roads we finished the ironing & mended & sewed
19

19

Emma's diary on the day of Michael's heart attack. Note that the bottom half of the page is for the year of 1956.

Starting School

When Arlene started school, she was not sure if she enjoyed it. Fortunately, she came down with a "convenient" ailment, and the teacher sent her home. This happened numerous times. On one of these midday walks home, she noticed Michael working in the field and would pass right along the edge of the road just as she would walk past. Not wanting her father to see her, she laid down in the grass until Michael was past. Unfortunately, she failed to look at the vegetation and laid right in a big patch of poison ivy. The results and sufferings surfaced a few hours later, and she had a legitimate reason to stay home from school.

Heart Attack!!

Michael was not feeling well in early 1955. On January 16 1955, he and Emma stayed home from church because he felt sick. In the afternoon, Melvins, Weavers and Johns visited. That evening at 6:30 p.m., Michael had a severe heart attack. Later at 9:00 p.m., he had another spasm and the doctor called the ambulance to take him to the hospital.

The hospital placed Michael in an oxygen tent to ease his breathing. In those days, a person who needed extra oxygen was placed in a plastic tent-

Michael and Emma's retirement home, built in 1956.

Michael and Emma's farm in the 1960s.

like structure instead of having tubes hooked up to them as it is done today. This made visiting difficult. He slowly recovered somewhat, and then had a backset. Emma visited him every day with the boys and neighbors taking her.

Life does go on even if father is in the hospital. The tobacco had to be stripped. Emma helped the boys fill the tobacco cellar before she went to see her husband in the hospital. About a week after Michael was admitted to the hospital, Emma changed their checking account to a joint account. Michael had done all monetary matters before this. The butcher came to butcher their pig and some of the tobacco was delivered to the buyer.

On February 12, 1955, Michael returned home, after almost a month in the hospital, but was confined to bed. I remember to this day visiting him that evening. We had strict orders to play quietly on the kitchen floor. We children were allowed to go into the sick room for a short time. I expected to see a washed-out and feeble old grandfather, but was pleasantly surprised when he entertained us with a pair of magnetic puppies. Michael placed one of the puppies under his bed sheet, hidden from us and placed the other one on the upper side of the bed sheet where we could see it. By moving the hidden puppy, he could make the other puppy run around on the top of the bed sheet.

Emma's mother passed away over this time and due to his condition, Michael stayed home. The family came and read her will at Michael and Emma's home because Michael was confined to the house.

Towards the end of February, Michael was walking out to the barn. On March 30, 1955, he had more heart spasms. The doctor came and ordered him back to bed, saying if he gets any worse, he will need to return to the hospital. After another two weeks of bed confinement with the doctor visiting every day, he slowly improved.

Michael's condition was up and down. One day when he was having a poor day, Emma felt it warranted a call to the doctor. They tried to call him but were unsuccessful. Leon was sitting in the house when he spotted Doctor Lauria's car coming down the road. He raced out on the porch and waved frantically. At the last instant, the Doctor saw him and slid to a stop. He backed up, turned into the lane, inquired what was needed, and tended to Michael's condition.

During this time, Leon and Frank had to take responsibility of the farm. The cows and chickens could not wait. They finished stripping tobacco, and got the tobacco bed ready for next year's crop. They shouldered the new responsibility willingly and did their duties well. However, they did not have the years of experience that Michael had. In those days, the corn was shocked in the field. After the corn was husked by hand, the fodder was brought to the barn and stacked outside for cattle feed and bedding. However, in order for it to keep, the fodder had to be stacked in a way that it shed water. If it got wet, it would mold and spoil.

Apparently, the stack got wet and with warmer weather, it was too moldy to use. Frank and Leon started to haul the moldy corn fodder to the edge of the field and burn it. A few days later, Raymond, Lloyd, and Weaver, brought their families for a visit. They decided to burn this spoiled feed before Michael would find out about it. They started a fire and brought the wagon loaded with the spoiled fodder alongside the fire. Apparently, they parked too close to the fire, and the loaded wagon also started to burn. They energetically tipped the entire wagon so that the fodder would slide off. However, when the wagon was on its side, it got away from them and fell into the fire. They thought maybe the whole load of fodder, plus the wagon on top of it would smother the fire. Raymond who was on the tractor tried to pull the wagon off, put was unsuccessful. Leon ran for the barn and got the fire extinguisher. Everyone was excited and unorganized.

Finally, all the men become organized, righted the wagon, and pulled it away from the fire. Leon then extinguished the fire on the wagon, which was damaged, but still usable.

Leon was the oldest boy at home, so much of the farming responsibilities fell on him. When it was time to plant corn, he did not feel confident to use Michael's horse-drawn planter. Henry Huber offered the use of his Farmall C with a two-row corn planter. Leon accepted this offer, and with some instruction from Henry, Leon planted corn for the first time.

Due to Michael's condition, plans were made to build a new house on the southeast corner of the farm along Route 625. John and Alverta were to take over the farm. Michael was still going to take care of the chickens. Gathering and grading the eggs gave him something to do and provided some additional income.

Michael was also involved in canning meat for relief. When he retired from the farm, he scheduled the volunteer help on this project. He was responsible to make sure enough people would finish the job properly. This also included providing transportation for some of the team people.

Michael also had another talent which ensured that he had a personal contact with his boys and grandsons. Many of his sons came home after they were married to get their haircuts. Some of Michael's grandsons would also sit on his stool with a towel wrapped around his shoulders getting a haircut. Many of the grandsons can attest that Michael was not above giving a stern, "Be still," along with a stiff nudge when they began to get restless.

Michael and Emma's retirement years were full and fulfilling. They were

Michael Burkholder in 1982.

active in church work. Michael attended many of the ministry conferences as a visitor. They traveled with Deacon Henry Martin and Bishop Joseph Weaver to distant states as the church leaders attended their duties. Each communion, Emma washed some of the towels used in the sacred services of feet washing, and returned them to Deacon Henry Martins. Michael was the book holder for the churches' fire aid plan. This meant attending meetings and work each time a brother had a loss.

Fridays were usually spent at Green Dragon shopping for groceries and visiting with friends. Usually they would also stop at the Acme Market in Ephrata to pick up what they could not buy at Green Dragon. Michael kept a keen interest in the dairy business and was a regular patron at the New Holland Cow Sale every Wednesday. When his sons remodeled their barns or homes, you could count on Michael and Emma frequently dropping in to check on the progress.

Michael also took care of the chickens down on the farm. He hand-gathered the eggs into wire egg baskets and carried them up to the stripping room. There he graded each egg individually and cleaned those needing it, and packed them in thirty-dozen boxes. I can still see him sitting on a stool in a corner of the stripping room inspecting each egg. He took a dirty egg and pressed it against a sanding wheel, twirling the egg until the offending smudge was gone, and placed it on an egg flat. Michael placed the packed, cleaned, and graded eggs, in the cool tobacco cellar to await pickup by the egg man.

The Martin birds and the garden were also a special delight to Michael and Emma. Michael's lawn was nurtured, trimmed, weeded, and fertilized. It was an uninterrupted lush green carpet of green grass mowed to perfection, compared to the lawn his boys mowed at home.

Visiting and visitors also occupied much of their time. Canadian friends were frequent visitors. Friends and relatives dropped in. Many of the grandchildren came for an extended stay, plus babysitting, while the parents had appointments. As the end of March approached, there was always the flurry of visitors with "April Business," which was both expected and appreciated.

Each Christmas all of Michael and Emma's children came home, bringing all the grandchildren to enjoy a Christmas dinner. Michael usually sat at the head of the table. As a young lad, I can recall my brother,

• 103 •

Ray and I sitting around each corner from his lofty position. Cranberry salad was a new thing, and Grandma was serving it for the first time. Never having tasted it and not knowing what it was, Ray decided to pass it by, and passed the serving dish to Michael. "What, no cranberry salad?" remarked Michael as he plopped a generous helping on Ray's plate. After taking a serving for himself, he passed the dish to me. Being in the same ignorant shoes as Ray, I took a small helping, fearing the serving dish would be called back. Oh, by the way, today we both enjoy cranberry salad.

Michael drove a 1957 Oldsmobile which he used as his good Sunday car to go down to the farm when the weather was not suitable to ride a bike or walk. He drove this car until 1961 when he purchased a new Oldsmobile Dynamic. Michael did not feel good about going down to the farm, feeding the chickens, gathering the eggs and then smelling up his new Oldsmobile. He also recognized the short runs were not beneficial for the longevity of his car. Two weeks later, he purchased a used Volkswagen beetle with a red interior, for use during the week. Shortly after he had the Volkswagen, a church brother mentioned that his black beetle looked sharp with its chrome bumpers and red interior. The offending bumpers were taken care of, and Michael had a form of dependable transportation that everyone in the community could recognize instantly.

Apparently, Michael enjoyed driving his little VW because a few years later he traded it in for a brand new one.

On February 22, 1966, Michael and Emma, and Sam Good and his wife took an extended trip south. Visiting numerous lumberyards on their way south, they arrived in Florida two days later. Michael enjoyed numerous fishing trips with Edwin Nolt while the ladies went shopping. After enjoying the sights and weather in Florida for three weeks, they traveled to Atmore, Alabama, visiting Martin Weber. However, it felt good to arrive home after the extended trip.

Despite all of Michael's extended activities in the school board and the fire aid plan, photographs of him are extremely rare. Michael had strong convictions on the photograph. On one occasion, one of Michael's granddaughters had both of her grandparents at home for a meal. In the afternoon, she expressed her desire to take some pictures of her grandparents. Michael refused with the remark, "I had a picture taken at the age of eighteen and have regretted it ever since."

In his later years, Michael was asked to say the table blessing with an audible prayer. His reply was that since he prays in German, the others present would not understand him and with this logic, he refused. Years later he remarked that he regretted that decision, and lamented that his children never heard him pray audibly.

Michael also enjoyed going down to the banks of the Conestoga to fish. When his grandson, Harold Burkholder, and his friend, Wilmer Hurst, asked Michael, to teach them how to fish, he had time and patience to fulfill their desire. The hobby of fishing also led to numerous fishing trips to the Chesapeake Bay. John and Alverta usually arranged the details and Michael went with them. John Rutt, Alverta's father, who also enjoyed fishing, usually was there as well.

Nevertheless, this earth is not our eternal abode and all flesh is bound for the grave. Emma struggled with arthritis in her later years. It appears that Emma realized that her struggle with her life was ending. As Leon took his Mother to the hospital, she remarked, "This might be the beginning of the end." Leon tried to encourage her by disagreeing, mentioning future grandchildren and great-grandchildren. Michael interrupted saying, "If she is preparing to move into eternity, please let hee alone."

Later Michael told Leon about the symptoms and pain that Emma was experiencing that the rest of the family knew nothing about. It appears that Michael also realized his partner was about to leave him for a heavenly home. Later when Bishop Joseph Weaver visited her, Emma asked him to pray for her, but not that she would get better. After spending three weeks in Ephrata Community Hospital, she went home to the Lord on August 16, 1971.

The funeral was held at Weaverland Mennonite Church. Phares Martin had the gravesite services and the mourners sang, "Going Down the Valley," as the grave was closed. Aaron Horning and Joseph Weaver had the services in the church. Most of Aaron Horning's service was in German at Michael's request.

Life, however, goes on and Michael came home to an empty home. He took many of his meals with Melvin and Arlene down on the farm. His daughters and daughter-in-laws also did much of the housecleaning. Michael also took up a new hobby while he was a widower. He started to cut patches and purchased a new sewing machine to piece them.

Hurricane Agnes

In 1972, a severe hurricane swept through eastern Pennsylvania. Hurricane Agnes dumped a deluge of water over the county with severe flooding in many parts.

Near the village of Pool Forge, where Route 23 crosses the Conestoga River, flooding was severe, making the road impassable. The owner of the Pool Forge mansion, a ninety-year-old lady, and her care-taker were surrounded, and stranded by the floodwaters. The police and firemen came with a boat to rescue them. They rescued the ladies, taking them out of the second-story window of the adjoining carriage house into a motorboat. However, as they went toward land and safety, the boat struck a submerged fence post, breaking the propeller. With no propeller, the boat lost control in the flood waters, and capsized, dumping all of them into the water. The firemen focused rescuing the ninety-year-old lady, hoisting her and tying her into a tree until they could reorganize the rescue effort. The ladies' caretaker struggled back to the carriage house on her own where they originally had been stranded. The firemen eventually got the elderly lady back into the house with the caretaker. After this trying experience, the elderly lady had to calm her nerves with a nip of sherry.

The firemen were at a loss as to what to do. Their boat was damaged and worthless in the raging torrent, and the ladies were still stranded in the carriage house.

Frank Weaver, a local farmer heard the commotion on his police moni-tor. He went out to the scene and talked to John Gehman, the local police officer. Frank looked over the scene and suggested that he felt that he could reach the carriage house with his combine. The police officer said it was worth a try, and Frank went home to get his combine. Frank took his combine through the deep water, drove up to the carriage house, and rescued the two women. They all squeezed into the combine cab and drove out to safety.

Watching all of this action from the other side of the raging and impassable Conestoga River was Michael Burkholder. The caretaker of this ninety-year-old lady was Anna H. Martin who Michael was dating, and whom he had legitimate concerns for the safety of his fiancée. Appar-ently, the call Anna made to the fire company for assistance was not the only place she went for help.

Michael and Anna were married on July 22, 1972. Anna was the widow of Reuben W. Martin and had three children with her first husband. Noah, Mary, and Ruth, were added to the family circle. Noah was married, and Mary was engaged, planning to be married that fall. But Ruth brought a teenager into Michael's life again.

Serenaded

That Sunday night, Michael and Anna had unexpected visitors. Apparently some of Michael's children foresaw this could happen. Raymond warned his daughter, Ruth Ann, that she is not allowed to go serenade her grandfather. However, that evening Ruth Ann and her friends were sitting around deciding what to do, when one of the girls mentioned that Michael and Anna just got married. Instantly one of the other girls suggested serenading him later in the evening. With eight other girls, Ruth Ann was out-voted. However, before going, they went to play volleyball, and other youth joined in the plans to serenade Michael and Anna. At about dusk, they drove and parked near the turkey farm and walked the rest of the way. Ruth Ann told the group where their bedroom window was located, and then ran over to Conestoga Wood Products and hid behind the bushes. The group of young people made a racket and soon the bedroom lights came on. Shortly, the back door opened and the group of young people were invited to come in.

Michael and Anna stood by the laundry door and watched them file in one by one. After they were all in, Michael peeked out the door and remarked that he expected to see another person he knew. The young people were served

Michael and Anna Burkholder in 1987.

Children of Michael W. and Emma Burkholder: Melvin, Raymond, Arlene, Lloyd, Frank, Titus, Leon, John, and Weaver. Edna is absent.

a treat and they had a nice little visit. The generation gap was bridged to the satisfaction of all involved, and Ruth Ann did not have to disobey her parents.

    Anna had a quilt business and Michael was soon heartily involved in this venture. First, he only cut the patches, but soon Michael and Anna each had their own sewing machines humming at piecing quilts. Michael also quilted, but as he aged, he was no longer able to craft the fine stitching required for a saleable quilts. Anna permitted Michael to quilt to his heart's content, but redid some of his stitching when he was not there.

    Michael had more interest in the lawn than the garden, but Anna has a "green thumb" when it comes to gardening. If the weather did not cooperate with rain, the lawn needed watered before the garden. The lawn was treated to kill the weeds, and if any stray dandelions were seen, they were soon removed; hands and knees on the ground with a weeding trowel. After Michel's health no longer enabled him to do this, Anna had to take over this chore.

    Michael still had his chickens down on the farm until it was sold to Conestoga Wood Products in 1975. The weekly trip to Green Dragon market continued even if there was nothing to purchase. Anna feared for his safety when he went fishing along the Conestoga, fearing he would fall in, but it never happened.

The grandchildren's weddings were faithfully attended, even those in Missouri, where Edna and Lloyd Martin had made their home.

Michael passed away on June 1, 1988, at the Ephrata Hospital. He was alert to the end. Anna had been staying with him day and night. Raymond had come in for a morning visit, giving Anna an opportunity to go home to shower, nap, and change clothes.

While Michael and Raymond were visiting, a nurse came in and cleared the lungs of Michael's roommate with a suction device. Michael was also receiving this procedure and he despised it. Knowing he was next, Michael told Raymond saying, "I don't have to go through this." He turned his back to the approaching nurse, and changed time for eternity. He was buried at the Weaverland Mennonite Church Cemetery with Bishop Joseph Weaver and Amos Martin officiating. A popular and well-liked patriarch was laid into eternal rest, a pattern for all who remember him to follow.

◆ *Chapter Seventeen* ◆

Michael Burkholder's Ancestors

What stories could have been told by those in generations before the printed word became so accessible! If only more stories would have been recorded about the hopes and trials for the benefit of future generations. However, most of the everyday trials and struggles have been lost. It is needful, however, to show a short excerpt of the Burkholder linage, starting with Michael Burkholder's grandfather and going back as far as remembered.

Daniel S. Burkholder

John W. Burkholder, Michael's father, was the third child of Daniel S. Burkholder (1833-1915), and married Anna Burkholder (Weaver), on December 1, 1857. They had twelve children and were farmers in nearby Martindale, Lancaster County.

Living in a time when the English language was making strong inroads, Daniel made strong efforts to teach his children the particulars of his mother tongue. His children were taught the traditional German prayers and strongly encouraged to memorize a thirty-one-stanza song found in *Unparttheyisches Gesang-Buch*. Daniel was slightly hard of hearing, but he made up for this handicap, by his sharp eyes and acute perception. It is remembered that as the evening grew late, he would call the boys in with the saying, "Come in; sometimes there is conversation that isn't good."

Daniel was a strong and rugged man, and well-noted for his strength. He had bright blue eyes, black hair combed with no part, with bangs on his forehead—the plainest of hairstyles.

Daniel could write German and English script equally well, and was a well-respected man in the community. He was very concerned about the light that his life left in the community. For years, he refrained from buying a dinner bell so his wife could call the family for meals because he remembered opposition to bells from earlier generations. He also shunned the new factory-made dark-colored material used to make shirts and kept wearing his old fashioned white homespun shirts. When his wife objected to the daily washing and bleaching, he remarked, "I was taught this way, and must I wear a dark shirt in my old years?" Daniel was slow to accept change. Daniel's son, David, refused to accept the $10 customarily given to buy a saddle, because it was now a common practice to ride in a buggy instead of riding a horse. Daniel deducted that amount from the financial help usually received at marriage.

Daniel was ordained as an assistant deacon on August 25, 1864. He served as a deacon when the Mennonite church was under pressure to accept Sunday school. Bishop Jonas Martin, and Deacon Daniel Burkholder, and other conservative members, continued to hold to the older ways, viewing Sunday school as a worldly offering.

Daniel went with the Jonas Martin group in the church division in 1893, and served his congregation for 51 years. As the longest serving deacon he always strived for the plainest lifestyle

John W. Burkholder

Daniel S. Burkholder was the third child of John W. Burkholder (1807-1862) and Esther Burkholder Sauder (1807-1850). John had nine children—two from a second marriage—and farmed, living in Lancaster County. Pennsylvania. They lived on an isolated farm in a long lane near the spot where the Muddy Creek flowed into the Conestoga Creek, northeast of Hinkletown. They attended Groffdale Mennonite Church until 1854 when Martindale Mennonite Church was built.

In 1845, the Pike Mennonite Church separated from the main church desiring a stricter discipline, and for a time, John and Esther were undecided which group they wanted to support. Over this time, John was voted into the lot for the ministry at the Pike Church, but he declined the vote and gave his support to the Old Order Mennonite Church.

• 111 •

Abraham Burkholder

John W. Burkholder was the seventh son of Abraham Burkholder (1768-1840). Abraham married Bishop Peter Eby's sister, Catherine (1771-1856). They had ten children and farmed on the homestead in West Earl Township. Abraham was ordained as a minister at Groffdale at about the age of forty. Preaching was difficult for him, and at his request and with congregational approval, he was appointed as deacon ten years later.

Immigrant Christian Burkholder

The life of Christian Burkholder is a vivid example of a Spirit-filled life that can be a model for all.

Abraham Burkholder was the son of immigrant Christian Burkholder, who came to America as a nine-year-old boy. His 49-year-old mother, Barbli, and five brothers and sisters arrived in Philadelphia in September 1754 on the ship *Phoenix*. Their father, Ulrich, had passed away after the trip was planned, but before the departure date arrived. They settled on the lands of Hans Groff, the notable pioneer near Groffdale, Lancaster County.

On February 15, 1761, Christian, a fatherless fifteen-year-old youth, recorded these remarkable words on his newly-purchased *Martyrs Mirror.*

> *"This Martyr book belong to me,*
> *Christian Burkholder,*
> *and I have bought it for my own use,*
> *and my souls salvation, ...*
> *and it cost me one pound and 17 shillings."*

Christian Burkholder later married Anna, granddaughter of Hans Groff and daughter of Daniel Groff. They started farming in 1766 on Daniel Groff's farm of 151 acres, which they purchased in 1770.

Christian was ordained as a minister in 1770 at the age of twenty-four, and as bishop in 1778. This was right in the midst of the turbulent years preceding the Revolutionary War, where the United States as we know it today, was struggling for freedom. The call to arms, the fighting mood of the people did not escape Lancaster County, or the nonresistant faith of the Mennonites.

In this time the Lancaster countryside rang with recruiters' drums calling for men to enlist and drill for war. Friction erupted between those who responded to the call to arms, and the Mennonites and some others who did not. Both sides became critical of the other. Two Mennonite ministers approached the Revolutionary Committee and reported their people were being harassed. A handbill was produced calling for moderation, but those drilling for "the business of war" took this handbill, attached it to the Lancaster Square whipping post, and shot it to pieces. Eventually the problem was solved with those who failed to volunteer, by paying a subscription, or a tax. This tax was reported as going to help the poor, but there was concern that it was really helping the war. At the head of the list of Earl Township's 108 individuals who were taxed for refusing to drill in the "arts of war," was young preacher Christian Burkholder's name!

In 1792, Christian wrote an extensive book, *Address to Youth*, printed in 1804, which is still used today in many Mennonite and Amish churches. He was a remarkable church leader whose influence spread far into neighboring counties. He passed away in 1809 at the age of 63.